Treatise on Death

TREATISE ON DEATH

Myles Coverdale

A facsimile version of Bishop Myles Coverdale's translation of the German work of Otho Wermullerus, circa 1550.This is the Parker Society edition, edited by George Pearson, B.D., and printed in 1846 at The University Press in Cambridge, England.

THE MISSION OF Baruch House Publishing, founded by editor Ruth Magnusson (Davis), is to bring to the world again the lost works of the early English Reformation. Our main focus is the 1537 Matthew Bible, and our ongoing work is to gently update it for readers today, with reference to the editor's own 1549 edition of the Matthew Bible. The Matthew Bible was the joint work of William Tyndale (c.1491-1536), Myles Coverdale (c.1487-1569), and John Rogers (c.1500-1555). It is the only English Bible that was bought with blood: both Tyndale and Rogers were burned at the stake for their work.

Baruch House has also undertaken to re-publish individually the best of Myles Coverdale's treatises and small books in an attractive, easy-to-read format, including:

Hope of the Faithful. A defence of the traditional doctrine of heaven and hell. An appendix shows how the change from "hell" to "Sheol" and "Hades" in the 1894 Revised Version of the Bible defeated the traditional doctrine.

Fruitful Lessons. Upbuilding teaching and instruction on the Passion, Death, Resurrection and Ascension of Christ, and of the sending of the Holy Spirit.

Treatise on Death. Deep and profound teachings on how to prepare for our own death, deal with those who are dying, and comfort the bereaved.

A Sweet Exposition on Psalm 23. Restoring the lost teaching that in Psalm 23 David was praising the word of God as the pasture and refreshing drink of God's sheep and the table set before them in the presence of their enemies.

A Spiritual and Most Precious Pearl. Why Christians should embrace the cross as a most sweet and necessary thing for the soul, what comfort to take from it, and how to find aid in afflictions.

TREATISE ON DEATH

Bishop Myles Coverdale, circa 1550. This edition 1846.

From *Remains of Myles Coverdale,*
published by the Parker Society.

The Society was "Instituted A.D. M.DCCC.XL for
the publication of the Works of the Fathers and Early Writers
of the Reformed English Church."

EDITED FOR

The Parker Society,

BY THE

REV. GEORGE PEARSON, B.D.

RECTOR OF CASTLE CAMPS,

AND LATE CHRISTIAN ADVOCATE IN THE UNIVERSITY OF CAMBRIDGE.

CAMBRIDGE:

PRINTED AT

THE UNIVERSITY PRESS.

M.DCCC.XLVI.

Scripture quotations in the Publisher's Foreword are from
the 2021 October Testament, the New Testament of the New Matthew Bible.

Cover design by Iryna Spica

ISBNs Canada:
Paperback 978-1-7771987-6-3
Hardcover 978-1-7771987-7-0

About the cover

The artwork on the front cover is a detail from *The Death of the Virgin,* an oil-on-oak painting by the Flemish artist Hugo van der Goes. Completed between 1470-80, it is considered to be one of van der Goes' last works and is housed in the treasury of St. Salvatore's Cathedral in Bruges. The full painting shows the Virgin Mary on her deathbed surrounded by the twelve apostles. Peter is holding the burning candle while another apostle cups the flickering flame in his hand. The flame has just been caught by a gust of air, which some link to the appearance of Christ above Mary's bed to receive her soul at the moment of her death.

Table of Contents

Publisher's Foreword

MYLES COVERDALE TRANSLATED his *Treatise on Death* from the German work of Otho Wermullerus (or Vuerdmullerus), a Reformer and scholar of Zurich, circa 1550. He translated three other works of Wermullerus at about the same time; these were *A Spiritual and Most Precious Pearl, Of Justification*, and *The Hope of the Faithful*.

Over the years of his long and productive life, before he died in 1569 and in addition to giving the world its first printed English Bible, Coverdale also translated other foreign authors, including Martin Luther and Heinrich Bullinger, and he wrote his own essays. Almost three centuries later the Parker Society undertook to reprint the major works of the English Reformation in modern spelling and published Coverdale's translations, personal writings, correspondence, and prologues to the Bible in two large volumes. Our facsimile of the *Treatise on Death* is taken with gratitude from the Society's 1846 volume, *Remains of Myles Coverdale*.

Coverdale's English is a little more obscure in the *Treatise on Death* than in his other works, but the glossary attached as Schedule A at the end of this volume will assist with obsolete words. However, some of the obscurity seems due to a more literal translation style than was Coverdale's usual custom, such as where, concerning the need to treat every day as if it might be our last, he wrote, "Learn to beware by the example of other men, upon whom stretch-leg came suddenly and slew them." Who or what is stretch-leg? It translates the German word "Streckbein," literally stretch-leg. The Oxford English Dictionary gives the figurative meaning "death," which is fitting, but shows Coverdale's *Treatise* as the sole example of use. Another non-English usage is "footstep" in the sentence, "When father and mother dieth, the son and the daughter remembereth how many a footstep the elders went faithfully and worthily to provide them their living." In other words, in English idiom, the children remember how many steps the parents took, or how far they went, to care for them. Coverdale lived many years in Germany, so German and English idioms no doubt became a little blurred in his mind.

The *Treatise on Death* sometimes refers to the articles of the Christian faith, which the author did not define but by which he almost certainly meant the tenets of the Apostles' Creed. The Creed is traditionally divided into twelve articles, which are set forth in Schedule B for reference.

THIS LITTLE BOOK lives up to the promise in the preface that, although it may appear a "small and slender a gift … yet it is neither little, nor to be despised, for the fountain's sake that floweth out of it, and by reason of the matter whereof it is written." The matter whereof it is written is death, which it discusses wisely, practically, and in the spirit of true faith.

Some things it says may seem a little foreign to us. This is partly because our times are so different. Progress in medicine has helped us cope much better with the diseases and ailments of which the author complains, and, in the West at least,

Christians have known relative prosperity and peace from persecutions. However, the times are changing, and it may happen sooner rather than later that we will also say:

> The universal trouble is manifold and piteous, specially now at this present time, with noisome diseases, divisions, wars, seditions, uproars. Like one water-wave follows upon another, and one can scarcely avoid another, even so oft-times comes one mischance in another's neck. In this short life to have no trouble for only one day is great advantage. (English gently updated in this and the quotations below from the *Treatise*.)

In the writings of the early 16th century, one often finds life on this earth described as piteous or wretched, or as a "vale of misery." In prosperity we may be tempted to dismiss this sentiment, but when misery comes, so does understanding.

However, it was not only diseases, divisions, and uproars that contributed to misery in Coverdale's time, but also a prevalent cruelty and barbarity. In the *Treatise on Death* mention is made of death "upon the wheel." This wheel went by several names, including "Catherine wheel" (after Saint Catherine of Alexandria, a young martyr who was tortured on it in the Middle Ages), "breaking wheel," and "execution wheel." It was a public torture and execution instrument, used primarily in Europe from antiquity through the Middle Ages and into the Early Modern Period. However, later uses included executions in New York and Louisiana in the 18th century during slave rebellions, and in Germany even into the 19th century. Criminals were tied to the wheel and tortured by various methods or bludgeoned to death. Victims would sometimes suffer prolonged agony on the wheel for several days.

More positively, we not infrequently find in early 16th-century writings references to a godly fear of the final judgment. This fear was part of popular religious culture and had been for centuries. Therefore Coverdale was able to write:

> Many people through fear of death give alms, exercise charity, and do their business circumspectly. To be short, the consideration of death is as a scourge or spur that encourages onward. It gives a man cause and occasion to avoid eternal death, whereof the death of the body is but a shadow [type or example].

However, nowadays we find little or no fear of the judgment, not even in the churches. For lack of this spur, people do not fear the consequences of sin and govern themselves accordingly. This lends credence to Tyndale's prophecy in his prologue to 2 Peter where he wrote, "In the latter days the people, through unbelief and lack of fear of the judgment of the last day, will be even as Epicures, wholly given to the flesh.... At the last, people will believe nothing, and not fear God at all." A great benefit of Coverdale's treatise is that it provides the spur people need – including Christians, in whom the flesh still lusts contrary to the Spirit – to live chaste and holy lives, ever mindful of the coming judgment. It is a necessary reminder that everything we do in this life prepares us for eternity.

This reminder, this spur, is conspicuously absent from Christian writing and preaching today, which only too often exhorts to complacency about sin. It is shameful even to speak of preaching that glories in slogans like, "Christianity is not about turning from vice to virtue," which I have heard several times. This ungodly slogan strikes at the first pillar of Christianity, which is repentance. Jesus began his ministry calling to the people, "Repent, for the kingdom of heaven is at hand" (M't. 4:17). John Rogers' note on this verse in the 1537 Matthew Bible explained, "To repent is to think again, and to change their evil life for the love of virtue and hate of sin." The slogan also strikes at the heart of conversion and the new birth, which is a very turning from sin to holiness – that is, from vice to virtue – and denies the call for holy fruit in the life of a believer:

> **1 Thessalonians 4:7-8** God has not called us to uncleanness, but to holiness. Whoever therefore rejects this, rejects not man, but God, who has sent his Holy Spirit among you.
>
> **1 Peter 1:3-9** His divine power has given to us all things that pertain to life and godliness ... so that by the help of them you may be partakers of the divine nature, in that you flee the corruption of worldly lust.
>
> And give all diligence to this. To your faith add virtue, and to virtue knowledge, and to knowledge temperance, and to temperance patience, to patience godliness, to godliness brotherly kindness, to brotherly kindness love. For if these things be among you and abound, they will make you so that you will neither be idle nor unfruitful in the knowledge of our Lord Jesus Christ. But he who lacks these things is blind, and gropes for the way with his hands, and has forgotten that he was purged from his old sins.
>
> **2 Corinthians 5:10-11** We must all appear before the judgment seat of Christ, so that every person may receive the works of his body, according to what he has done, whether it be good or bad.

ON ANOTHER NOTE, I will here add my comment to the Parker Society note respecting the opinion advanced on page 68 of the

Treatise that Holy Communion may only be practiced in the (public) coming together of a church. There it is stated:

> The sacrament of the body and blood of Christ must be exercised and practiced only in the coming together of the whole congregation and church, according to the example of the apostles. Therefore let the sick satisfy himself with the general breaking of bread whereof he was partaker with the whole congregation.

This begs the question as to the meaning of "congregation and church" and "the example of the apostles." It also appears not only to forbid Holy Communion to Christians who are sick and dying in the hospital, but any home or private communion at all, such as may be the only option for people who live under hostile, oppressive regimes. However, this does not appear to accord with Coverdale's own views. The Church of England, in which he served as a bishop, always allowed for communing the sick. Further, concerning the common spiritual authority and the priesthood of all believers, Coverdale generally agreed with Martin Luther, who repudiated sacerdotalism. It was partly to avoid appearances of sacerdotalism that Coverdale refused to wear any but the simplest of vestments when he served in the English Church. Luther wrote that, while good order requires the appointment of ministers to serve in public assemblies, the priesthood of believers permits the observance of communion to all equally, as well as other priestly functions:

> Here we take our stand: There is no other word of God than that which is given all Christians to proclaim. There is no other baptism than the one which any Christian can bestow. There is no other remembrance of the Lord's Supper than that which any Christian can observe and which Christ has instituted. There is no other kind of sin than that which any Christian can bind or loose. There is no

other sacrifice than of the body of every Christian. No one but a Christian can pray. No one but a Christian may judge of doctrine. These make the priestly and royal office.[1]

All things considered, including the general tenor of Coverdale's writing, the disallowance of private communion is most likely Wermullerus's opinion alone.

THE LAST ITEM in the *Treatise on Death*, the "Exhortation" written by Lady Jane Grey the night before she suffered, merits a comment. Lady Jane was the great granddaughter of Henry VII and a cousin of Edward VI. In his last Will and Testament, Edward nominated Lady Jane as his successor to the Crown, in part because she was a committed Protestant and would support the reformed Church of England. She reluctantly accepted and was proclaimed queen on July 10, 1553. However, the proclamation was disputed. Most of Jane's supporters then

---

[1] Martin Luther, "Concerning the Ministry," *Luther's Works,* American Edition, Volume 40 (Philadelphia: Fortress Press, 1958), 34-35. Luther wrote more largely here, "We have this word: 'For you have one master, Christ. You are all brethren (M't. 23: 8, 10).' We have then altogether the same rights. For if we have in common the name of brethren, then one cannot be especially superior to the other or enjoy more of heritage or authority than the other in spiritual matters, of which we now are speaking.... Since we have proved all of these things to be the common property of all Christians, no one individual can arise by his own authority and arrogate to himself alone what belongs to all. Lay hold then of this right and exercise it, where there is no one else who has the same rights. But the community rights demand that one, or as many as the community chooses, shall be chosen or approved who, in the name of all with these rights, shall perform these functions publicly. Otherwise, there might be a shameful confusion among the people of God, and a kind of Babylon in the church, where everything should be done in order, as the apostle teaches [1Co. 14: 40]. For it is one thing to exercise a right publicly, another to use it in time of emergency. Publicly one may not exercise a right without consent of the whole body or of the church. In time of emergency, each may use it as he deems best..." (33-35).

abandoned her, and suddenly, on July 19, 1553, the Privy Council changed course and proclaimed the Roman Catholic daughter of Henry VIII, Mary Tudor, as queen instead.

In the aftermath of this event, Jane was accused of treason and imprisoned in the Tower of London. She was convicted of high treason in November 1553 and died by beheading three months later, at the tender age of 17 – a brutal death after a harsh life. In the anxious night before her execution, she wrote the words of the *Exhortation* to her sister, Katherine, in the back of her Greek New Testament. Despite the circumstances, the words are sweet, mild, and not despairing. They attest to a noble character and a deep faith.

THE ENGLISH AT the beginning of the *Treatise on Death* is quite old-fashioned. To lead readers gently into the book, below is a lightly updated rendering of chapter 1, which is really no more than a short subsection. It offers foundational teaching and yields up wholesome new insight with each reading:

Chapter 1 of The First Book of Death

Declaring what death is

The Holy Scripture makes mention of four kinds of death and life.

1.   The first kind is called natural. The natural life subsists as long as the soul remains with the body upon earth. The natural death is that which separates the soul from the body.

2.   The second kind of death is a spiritual, unhappy death here in the time of life, when the grace of God, because of our wickedness, is departed from us. By the means of this

departing we are dead, separated from the Lord our God and from all goodness, though we still have the natural life. Contrary to this there is a spiritual, blessed life when we, through the grace of the Lord our God, live unto him and to all goodness. Saint Paul writes about this after this manner: "God, who is rich in mercy, through his great love with which he loved us even when we were dead in sins, has quickened us to life together in Christ."

3.   The third kind of death is a spiritual, blessed death here in time when the flesh, being continually and increasingly over time separated from the spirit [of the regenerate person], dies away from its own wicked nature. Contrary to this there is a spiritual, unhappy life, when the flesh with its wicked disposition continually breaks forth and lives in all wilfulness. Against this life Paul exhorts us, saying, "Mortify therefore your members that are upon the earth, fornication, uncleanness, unnatural lust, evil desires and affections, covetousness, etc."

4.   The fourth that the scripture makes mention of is an everlasting life and an everlasting death. Not that the body and soul of man will after this time lose their substance and be utterly no more. For we believe certainly that our soul is immortal, and that even this present body will rise again. But since we ourselves grant that life is sweet and death a bitter herb, this word life, by a figurative manner of speech, means mirth and joy. However, the word death is used to mean heaviness and sorrow. Therefore eternal life is called eternal joy, and eternal death is called eternal damnation.

Of these different types of deaths we commonly have a perverse judgment. We abhor the death of the body, and hasten on apace to the unhappy spiritual death, which is yet in itself a thousand times more terrible than any bodily death. For when a man delights in his own wickedness, though he yet still lives upon the earth he is nevertheless dead before God, and the soul must continue damned forevermore.

In this book I treat of the natural death, which before our eyes seems to be a complete destruction, and it seems that there is no help with the dead, even as when a dog or horse dies and God has no more respect to them. Yea, the world swims full of such ungodly people as have no other understanding. Otherwise, doubtless, they would conduct themselves differently towards God. In truth, death verily is not a destruction of man, but a deliverance of body and soul. Therefore, since the soul, being of itself immortal, does either out of the mouth ascend up into heaven or else from the mouth descend into the pit of hell, the body, losing its substance until doomsday, will then by the power of God be raised from death. It will then be joined again to the soul, so that afterwards the whole man with body and soul may eternally inherit either salvation or else damnation.

And so, as William Tyndale would say, go to now, dear reader. There is much to learn from this work. It manifests the profundity, poetry, faithful exaltation of Christ, and practical, godly simplicity that characterize the work of Myles Coverdale and Otho Wermullerus. R.M.D.

This facsimile book was prepared from a publication that is now almost 180 years old. Each page has received attention to correct imperfections arising from age, damage, or the scanning process. For the reader's convenience, the page numbers of the Table of Contents have been changed to accord with the numbering of this volume.

TREATISE ON DEATH.

℣ A most

frutefull piththye

and learned treatyse, how a chri

sten man oughte to behaue hym=

selfe in the dauger of death: and

how they are to bee releued and

comforted, whose deare frendes

are departed oute of this

worlde, moste necessary

for this our bnfortu=

nate age and sor=

rowefull

dayes.

☞John. 6.

Uerely verely, I saye bnto you,
he that beleueth in me, hath e=
uerlastynge lyfe.

PREFACE.

UNTO ALL THOSE THAT UNFEIGNEDLY DESIRE
TO LIVE UNDER THE FEAR OF GOD, AND WITH
PATIENCE ABIDE THE COMING OF OUR LORD
AND SAVIOUR JESUS CHRIST, THROUGH
THE WORKING OF THE HOLY
GHOST, GRACE AND PEACE
BE MULTIPLIED.

THOUGH all kinds of beasts have some things in common one with another, as in that they see, hear, feel, desire, move from one place to another; yet hath every beast also his own special property, as the bird hath another nature than the fish, the lion another disposition than the wolf. Even so in other my books, heretofore by me published, I have set forth a general comfort concerning trouble, sickness, poverty, displeasure, dearth, war, imprisonment, and death, under which I have comprehended all the cross and affliction of man. Nevertheless every mischance or adversity hath also his own special consideration: and forasmuch as among terrible things upon earth death is esteemed the most cruel of all, and it can yet with no wisdom of man be rightfully judged, how it goeth with a Christian in and after death; therefore the greatest necessity requireth, that we Christians be diligently instructed by the infallible word of God in especial, touching the end and conclusion of our life. For when the last hour draweth nigh, which we every day, yea, every twinkling of an eye look for; whether the soul after it be departed do live, whether the corrupted body shall rise again, whether eternal joy and salvation be at hand, and which way conducteth and leadeth to salvation; thereof hath the most subtle worldly-wise man by his own natural reason no knowledge at all. Plato, Aristotle, Cicero, the greatest-learned and wisest, write of these high weighty matters very childishly and foolishly[1]; and as for consolation that they give, it is in

[1 With respect to the opinions of the ancient philosopher on the immortality of the soul and a future state, those who wish to ex-

21

no sort nor wise to be compared unto the holy divine scripture, which only ministereth the true christian comfort in life
and death.   And though every man ought daily to consider
his end, and at all times to make himself ready for death,
seeing that he knoweth not how, where, and when God shall
lay his hand upon him ; yet nevertheless at this present time
we have more occasions to talk and treat thereof, now that
Almighty God doth with diverse and sundry plagues, more
grievously than heretofore, visit our unrepentant life, for that
he all this while hath perceived in us but little amendment;
neither need we to think, that these, that rain, and other
plagues shall over-leap us.   Considering now that I, though
unworthy and unmete, was called by authority, but specially
of God, to teach, to exhort, and to comfort ; I have, with
great labour, out of the holy scripture and out of old and
new authors collected, how a man should prepare himself unto
death, how he is to be used that lieth a dying, and how they[2]
ought to be comforted, whose dear friends are departed.
Which things, as they be orderly set in this book, right
dearly beloved and loving reader, I do present, dedicate, and
offer unto thee.   And though I can consider, that this little
book is so small and slender a gift, because of my person ;
yet is it neither little, nor to be despised, for the fountain's
sake that it floweth out of, and by reason of the matter
whereof it is written.   For herein out of the unchangeable
word of God are noted the head articles of our last conflict
and battery, whereupon dependeth either eternal victory,
honour, and joy, or else everlasting loss and endless pain; of
the which things we can never think, talk, nor treat sufficiently.   Wherefore, whereas this little book goeth forth unto
thy use, that art an unfeigned Christian, and to the comfort
of all such as are afraid of death ; I pray thee, for Christ's
sake, not only to accept it as the testimony of a willing and
loving mind toward thee, but also to have still an earnest
desire to that that it hath pleased God by me at this time to
communicate unto thee ; that with thy thankfulness thou

amine the subject may consult Bishop Warburton's Divine Legation,
Book III., where the opinions of the ancient philosophers are investi-
gated.]

[2 From this place to the end of the preface is supplied from the
Bodleian copy.]

mayest move other to the like, that can do better, and by thy
profit stir the harvest-lord to send more harvest-men into his
harvest. Which he cannot but do, except he could deny
himself, that came into the world, neither to
put out the flax that smoketh, nor to
break the reed that is but bruised,
but to open to them that knock
to him. Vale. Love God,
leave vanity, and
live in Christ.

THE TABLE.

THE CONTENTS OF THE FIRST PART.

24

THE CONTENTS OF THE SECOND PART.

THE CONTENTS OF THE THIRD PART.

FIRST BOOK OF DEATH.

CHAPTER I.

DECLARING WHAT DEATH IS.

HOLY scripture maketh mention of four manner of deaths and lives.

1. The first is called a natural life, so long as the soul remaineth with the body upon earth. The natural death is it that separateth the soul from the body.

2. The second is a spiritual unhappy death here in time of life, when the grace of God, for our wickedness' sake, is departed from us; by means whereof we were dead from the Lord our God and from all goodness, although as yet we have the life natural. Contrary unto this there is a ghostly blessed life, when we, through the grace of the Lord our God, live unto him and to all goodness. Hereof writeth St Paul after this manner: " God, which is rich in mercy, through his Eph. ii. great love wherewith he loved us, even when we were dead in sins, hath quickened us together in Christ."

3. The third is a ghostly blessed death here in time, when the flesh being ever, the longer the more, separated from the spirit, dieth away from his own wicked nature. Contrary hereunto is there a ghostly unhappy life, when the flesh with his wicked disposition continually breaketh forth, and liveth in all wilfulness. Against this doth Paul exhort us, saying: " Mortify therefore your members which are upon earth, for- Coloss. iii. nication, uncleanness, unnatural lust, evil concupiscence, covetousness, &c."

4. The fourth that the scripture maketh mention of, is an everlasting life, and an everlasting death. Not that the body and soul of man shall after this time lose their substance, and be utterly no more. For we believe undoubtedly, that our soul is immortal, and that even this present body

shall rise again.   But forasmuch as we ourselves grant that
life is sweet, and death a bitter herb, this word life by a
figurative speech is used for mirth and joy; this word
death, for heaviness and sorrow.   Therefore eternal life is
called eternal joy ; and eternal death eternal damnation.

Of these manifold deaths have we commonly a perverse
judgment. We abhor the death of the body, and haste on
apace to the unhappy ghostly death, which yet in itself is
a thousand times more terrible than any death corporal.   For
when a man delighteth in his own wickedness, though as yet
he live upon the earth, he is nevertheless dead before God,
and the soul must continue still damned for evermore.

In this book my handling is of natural death, which before our eyes seemeth to be an utter destruction, and that there
is no remedy with the dead, even as when a dog or horse
dieth; and that God hath no more respect unto them.   Yea,
the world swimmeth full of such ungodly people, as have
none other meaning.   Else, doubtless, would they behave
themselves otherwise towards God.   Death verily is not a
destruction of man, but a deliverance of body and soul.
Wherefore as the soul, being of itself immortal, doeth either
out of the mouth ascend up into heaven, or else from the
mouth descendeth into the pit of hell; the body, losing his
substance till doomsday, shall then by the power of God be
raised from death, and joined again to the soul; that afterward the whole man with body and soul may eternally inherit either salvation, or else damnation.

CHAPTER II.

THAT THE TIME OF DEATH IS UNCERTAIN.

THE body of man is a very frail thing.   Sickness may
consume it, wild beasts may devour it, the fire may burn it,
the water may drown it, the air may infect it, a snare may
choke it, the pricking of a pin may destroy it.   Therefore
when his temporal life shall end, he cannot tell.

The principal cause why we know not the time of death,

is even the grace of God; to the intent that we by no occa- Luke xii.
sion should linger the amendment of our lives until age, but
alway fear God, as though we should die to-morrow.

But as soon as the hour cometh, no man shall overleap
it. Hereof speaketh Job, when he saith, that "God hath Job xiv.
appointed unto man his bounds which he cannot go beyond."

CHAPTER III.

THAT IT IS GOD WHICH HATH LAID THE BURDEN OF DEATH UPON US.

IT becometh all Christians not only to suffer, but also to
commend and praise, the will of the heavenly Lord and
King. Now is it his will that we die. For if the sparrows,
whereof two are bought for a farthing, fall not on the ground
without God the Father, much less we men, whom God himself esteemeth to be of more value than many sparrows, yea,
for whose sakes other things were created, do fall to the
ground through death without the will of God: like as the
soldier tarrieth in the place wherein he is appointed of the
chief captain to fight against the enemies, and if he call him
from thence, he willingly obeyeth; even so hath the heavenly
Captain set us upon earth, where we have to fight, not with Ephes. vi.
flesh and blood, but with wicked spirits. Therefore if he give
us leave, and call us from hence, we ought by reason to obey
him. Like as one should not withdraw himself from paying
what he oweth, but gently to restore the money; so hath God
lent us this life, and not promised that we may alway enjoy
it. Therefore is death described to be the payment of natural debt.

CHAPTER IV.

THAT GOD SENDETH DEATH BECAUSE OF SIN.

ACCORDING hereunto ponder thou the just judgment of
God; for out of the third chapter of the first book of Moses
it is evidently perceived, that death is a penalty deserved,

31

laid upon us all for the punishment of sin. As the little worm that groweth out of the tree gnaweth and consumeth the tree of whom it hath his beginning; so death groweth, waxeth out of sin, and sin with the body it consumeth: and specially the venomous sickness which they call the pestilence, is sent of God as a scourge for the punishment of our naughtiness. Hereof speaketh the word of God in the fifth book of Moses Deut. xxviii. after this manner: " If thou wilt not hearken unto the voice of the Lord thy God, to keep and to do all his command-ments and ordinances, which I command thee this day, then shall all these curses come upon thee, and overtake thee: the Lord shall make the pestilence to cleave unto thee, until he have consumed thee from the land, whither thou goest to enjoy it. The Lord shall smite thee with swelling, with fevers, heat, burning, withering, with smiting and blasting. And they shall follow thee till thou perish."

2 Sam. xxiv. Yet among the most gracious chastenings is the pestilence reckoned of the holy prophet, and king David; who, after that he of a pride had caused the people to be numbered, when the election was given him, whether he would rather have seven years' dearth, three months' overthrow in war, or 1 Chron. xxii. three days' pestilence in the land, made this answer: " I am in a marvellous strait. But let me fall, I pray thee, into the hands of the Lord, for much is his mercy; and let me not 2 Sam. xxiv. fall into the hands of men. Then sent the Lord a pestilence 1 Chron. xxii. into Israel, that there died of them seventy thousand men." Wherefore, if God overtake thee with this horrible disease, be not thou angry with Saturnus and Mars, nor with the corrupt air and other means appointed of God; but be displeased with thine own sinful life. And when any fearful image of death cometh before thee, remember that thou with thy sins hast deserved much more horrible things, which God nevertheless hath not sent unto thee.

32

CHAPTER V.

THAT GOD TURNETH DEATH INTO GOOD.

ALTHOUGH thou hast deserved an hundred thousand greater plagues, yet shalt thou comfort thyself beforehand after this manner: A father doth his children good, and not evil. Now is my belief in God, as in my gracious Father, through Jesus Christ; and sure I am, that Christ upon the cross hath made a perfect payment for all my sins, and with his death hath taken away the strength of my death; yea, for me hath he deserved and brought to pass eternal life. Wherefore though death in the sight of my eyes and of natural reason be bitter and heavy; yet by means of the passion and death of Jesus Christ it is not evil or hurtful, but a benefit, a profitable and wholesome thing, even an entrance into everlasting joy.

CHAPTER VI.

THAT DEATH IN ITSELF IS GRIEVOUS TO THE BODY AND SOUL.

WHAT grief and hurt death doth bring with it, I will now declare, to the intent that when we have considered the same, before trouble come, we may in our distress be the less afraid, holding against it the great commodities of death that Christ hath obtained for all faithful. It grieveth a man at his death to leave the pleasant beholding of heaven and earth, his own young body and cheerful stomach, his wife and children, house and lands, fields and meadows, silver and gold, honour and authority, good friends and old companions, his minstrelsy, pastime, joy, and pleasure, that he hath had upon earth.

Afterward, when death knocketh at the door, then beginneth the greatest trouble to work. When the diseases be fallen upon the body of man in greater number, they are against all the members in the whole body, breaking in by heaps with notable griefs; so that the power of the body is weakened, the mind cumbered, the remembrance astonished, reason blinded, sleep hindered, the senses all-to broken: by means whereof the eyes are darkened, the face is pale, the feet are cold, the hands black, the members out of course, the brow hardened, the chin falleth down, the breath diminisheth, the deadly sweat breaketh out; yea, the whole man is taken in and disturbed, in such sort that he is now past minding any other thing. Death also is so much the more bitter and terrible, because that the feeble discomfited nature doth print the horrible image of death too deep in itself, and feareth it too sore. And hereunto is the devil likewise busy, to set before us a more terrible evil death than ever we saw, heard, or read of; to the intent that we, being oppressed with such imaginations or thoughts, should fly and hate death, and be driven to the love and carefulness of this life, forgetting the goodness of God, and to be found disobedient at our last end. Moreover, whoso of himself is not thoroughly assured, and knoweth yet sin by himself, he is not astonished for nought; forasmuch as sin carrieth with it the wrath of God and eternal damnation. Now not only the evil, but also the good, have grievous and manifold sins, (yea, more than they themselves can think upon,) with the which, in dangers of body and life, their mind is oppressed, as it were, with a violent water that fiercely rageth and gusheth out; yea, even the same praiseworthy and commendable thing which the godly have practised already, that do they yet perceive not to be perfect, but mixed with uncleanness. Hereof speaketh Isaiah in this wise: "We offend and have been ever in sin, and there is not one whole. We are all as an unclean thing, and all our righteousnesses are as filthy rags."

Isai. lxiv.

Psal. cxliii.
David prayed: "Lord, enter not into judgment with thy servant; for in thy sight shall no man living be justified."

Gregory writeth: "Woe unto the commendable life of men, if it be led without mercy!"

1 Pet. v.
Item, the apostle Peter giveth warning: "Your adversary, the devil, goeth about as a roaring lion, seeking whom he may devour."

If one that is about to shoot a gun be unsteady at the letting of it go, he misseth altogether, and all that he prepared for it before is in vain: even so, at the end of this life, are devils most busy to turn us from the right mark, that our former travail and labour may be lost; forasmuch as they know that there remaineth but a very small time of life; so that if the soul escape them now, they shall afterward go without it for evermore.

Even as mighty enemies do besiege and lay assault to a city, so the devils compass the soul of man with violence and subtlety, to take possession of the poor soul, to apprehend it, and bring it to hell. When we are yet in prosperity, the devils would have us to make but a small matter of it, as though we were in no danger to God-ward, albeit we blaspheme, be drunken, and commit whoredom, break wedlock, &c. But in the danger of death they bring forth those wicked sins in most terrible wise, putting us in mind of the wrath of God, how he in times past here and there did punish and destroy wicked doers,—to the intent that our souls might be hindered, snared, shut up, bound, and kept in prison from repentance and faith, and never to perceive any way how to escape and to be delivered; and by reason thereof wholly to despair, and to become the devil's portion.

Furthermore, good friends and companions are loth to depart asunder, specially such as are new knit and bound together one to another, as two married persons. Now is the body and soul nearest of all bound and coupled one to the other; but in the distress of death the pain is so great, that it breaketh this unity, and parteth the soul from the body: for the which cause a man at his death doth naturally sigh in himself. Good companions upon earth, though they depart one from another, have an hope to come together again; but when the soul once departeth from the body, it hath no power to return again to the body here in this time. Whereof Job giveth two similitudes: "A tree, if it be cut [Job xiv.] down, there is some hope yet, and it will bud and shoot forth the branches again. Likewise the floods, when they be dried up, and the rivers, when they be empty, are filled again through the flowing waters of the sea. But when man sleepeth, he riseth not again, until the heaven perish." This understand, that after the common course one cometh not again in this present life; one cannot die twice, and after death cannot a man accomplish any more that he neglected aforetime.

How goeth it now both with the body and soul after

death? As soon as the soul from the body is departed, the body is spoiled of all his powers, beauty, and senses, and become a miserable thing to look upon. Augustine saith: " A man that in his lifetime was exceeding beautiful and pleasant to embrace, is in death a terrible thing to behold[1]." How nobly and preciously soever a man hath lived upon earth, his body yet beginneth to corrupt and stink, and becometh worms' meat: by means whereof the world is of this opinion, that the body cometh utterly to nought for ever. The world also knoweth nothing concerning the immortality of the soul; and they which already believe that the soul is immortal, doubt yet whether it shall be saved; yea, they say plainly, it were good to die, if one wist what cheer he should have in yonder world. To them is death like unto a misty and dark hole, where one woteth not what will become upon him.

CHAPTER VII.

THAT WE ALL COMMONLY ARE AFRAID OF DEATH.

By means of the occasions aforesaid, certain heathen men have given uncomfortable and desperate judgments concerning the passage of death. In the poet Euripides, in *Orestes*[2], one

[1 The author appears to refer to the treatise entitled, *Exhortatio de salutaribus documentis;* which is falsely attributed to Augustine, and is given by the Benedictine editors on the authority of MSS. to Paulinus, bishop of Aquileia, A.D. 776; with whom Cave agrees. Hist. Lit. Vol. I. pp. 250, 495. "Dic mihi, quæso, frater mi, qualis profectus est in pulchritudine carnis? Nonne, sicut fœnum æstatis ardore percussum arescit, et paulatim decorem pristinum amittit? Et cum mors venerit, dic mihi, quæso, quanta remanebit in corpore pulchritudo? Tunc recognosces, quia vanum est, quod antea inaniter diligebas. Cum videris totum corpus intumescere, et in fœtorem esse conversum, nonne claudes nares tuas, ne sustineas fœtorem fœtidissimum? .... Ille est finis pulchritudinis carnis et oblectationis."—Augustin. Vol. IV. 254 D. Ed. 1541.]

[2 The passage is in the Iphigenia in Aulide, vv. 1250—2:

τὸ φῶς τόδ' ἀνθρώποισιν ἥδιστον βλέπειν·
τὰ νέρθε δ' οὐδέν. μαίνεται δ' ὃς εὔχεται
θανεῖν. κακῶς ζῆν κρεῖσσον ἢ θανεῖν καλῶς.]

36

saith: "It is better to live ill, than to die well." Which words are very unchristianly spoken. Yet are there found examples, even of holy men, that they had a natural fear of death. The holy patriarch Abraham, thinking that he stood in danger of death by reason of his wife's beauty, would rather suffer all that else was exceeding heavy and bitter. He judged it a smaller matter to call his wife his sister, than to be destroyed himself.

Hezekiah, an upright valiant king, when the prophet told him he should not live, was afraid of death, and prayed earnestly that his life might be prolonged. In the new Testament, when the Lord Jesus drew near to his passion and death, he sweat blood for very anguish, and said: "My soul is heavy even unto the death." And thus he prayed: "Father, if it be possible, take this cup from me." *Isai. xxxviii.* *Matth. xxvi.*

The Lord saith unto Peter: "Verily, verily, I say unto thee, When thou wast young thou girdedst thyself, and walked whither thou wouldest: but when thou art old, thou shalt stretch forth thine hands, and another shall gird thee, and lead thee whither thou wouldest not." Lo, Peter being excellently endowed with the Spirit of God, and stedfast in faith, had yet in his age a natural fear of death; for the Lord said unto him before, that another should lead him whither he would not. Therefore writeth Gregory not upright, when he saith: "If the pillars tremble, what shall the boards do? Or if the heavens shake for such fear, how will that be unmoved which is under?" That is, if famous saints did fear to die, it is much less to be marvelled at, when we poor Christians are afraid. *John xxi.*

Experience witnesseth how feebly we set ourselves against death. Many an old, or otherwise vexed man, can neither live nor die: for in his adversity he ofttimes wisheth death; and when death approacheth, he would rather suffer whatsoever else upon earth, if he might thereby escape death. Many of us have heard the gospel a long season, and studied it thoroughly, so to say; yet are we so afraid of the death of ourselves and of our friends, as though there were none other life more to look for; even like as they that be of Sardanapalus' sort do imagine, or else mistrust the promise, comfort, and help of God, as though he were not able, or would not succour and deliver us. Yea, some there be, that if death be but spoken of, they are afraid at it.

CHAPTER VIII.

THE COMMODITY OF DEATH, WHEN IT DELIVERETH US FROM THIS SHORT TRANSITORY TIME.

ALL the aforesaid disprofits and griefs do justly vanish, and are nothing esteemed, in comparison of these commodities, when death delivereth us from this ruinous miserable life, from all enormities and vicious people, and conducteth us to eternal joy and salvation: which thing shall hereafter be plainly declared.

First, a short, transitory, and shifting life ought not to make us sorry. Though this life had nothing else but pleasure, what is yet shorter and more in decay than the life of man? Half the time do we sleep out; childhood is not perceived; youth flieth away so, that a man doth little consider it; age creepeth on unawares, before it is looked for. We can reckon well, that when children grow, they increase in years and days; but properly to speak, in their growing are their days diminished. For let a man live threescore or fourscore years, look now, how much he hath lived of the same days or years, so much is abated of the time appointed.

A lively similitude. Is it not now a folly, that a man can consider how his wine diminisheth in the vessel, and yet regardeth not how his life doth daily vanish away?

Among all things most undurable and most frail is man's life, which innumerable ways may be destroyed. It is compared unto a candle-light, that of the wind is soon and easily blown out. *Psal. ciii.* A man in his time is as the grass, and flourisheth as a flower of the field; for as soon as the wind goeth over it, it is gone.

The heathen poet Euripides called the life of mortal men *Dieculam,* that is, *a little day.* But the opinion of Phalerius Demetrius is, that it ought rather to be called one point of this time. This similitude soundeth not evil among Christians. For what is the whole sum of our life, but even one point, in comparison of the eternity that undoubtedly *Psal. xc.* followeth hereafter? David himself saith, "that our years *Psal. cxliv.* pass away suddenly." "Man is like unto a thing of nought: his time goeth away as doth a shadow."

CHAPTER IX.

ANOTHER COMMODITY, WHEN DEATH DELIVERETH US FROM THIS MISERABLE LIFE-TIME.

OUR desire is to be free from all weariness and misery; yea, the more we consider this present wretched life, the less fear shall we have of death, which delivereth us from all mischances and griefs of this time: heaps of troubles happen unto us and unto other men, yea, to special persons and whole nations, in body, soul, estimation, goods, wives, children, friends, and native countries.

Bodily health is soon lost, but hard to obtain again; and when it is already gotten, the doubt is, how long it will continue. There be more kinds of diseases than the best learned physicians do know: among the same some are so horrible and painful, that if one do but hear them named, it maketh him afraid; as the falling sickness, the gout, frenzy, the sudden stroke, and such like. Besides sickness, a man throughout his whole life cometh into danger by a thousand means and ways. Consider, with how great carefulness the child is carried in the mother's womb; how dangerously it is brought forth into the world. The whole childhood, what is it else but a continual weeping and wailing? After seven years the child has his tutors and schoolmasters to rule him, and beat him with rods. When he is come to man's stature, all that he suffered in his youth doth he count but a small travail, in comparison of it that he now from henceforth must endure. The old man thinketh that he carrieth an heavy burden or mountain upon his neck. Therefore weigh well the miserable body and the miry sack of thy flesh towards thy helper, and be not so sore afraid of death, that easeth thee of this wretched carcase. According hereunto is the mind cumbered and vexed, through sickness and griefs of the body, by reason that the body and soul are joined together. And how precious a thing, I pray you, is our natural reason! Childhood knoweth nothing concerning itself. Young folks take vain and unprofitable things in hand, supposing all shall be gold, and consider neither age to come, neither yet death;

Man's whole life.

39

and, even as the common saying is, thus will the world be beguiled. Whereas a man, the longer he liveth, should ever be the more and more wise, it cometh oft to pass that the more he groweth in years, the more he doteth, and afterward becometh even a very child, yea, twice a child.

The disquiet-ness of man's life. The mind is tempted, the lust rageth, the hope deceiveth, heaviness vexeth, carefulness is full of distress, fear disquieteth; yea, the terror of death is more grievous than death itself. It cannot be expressed, how a man is sometimes plagued with worldly favour; afterward vexeth he himself with care of temporal things. Many one marreth himself with vice and wickedness, getteth him an evil conscience and a gnawing heart.

The virtuous also have their blemishes and temptations, which unto them are heavier and more hurtful than the blemishes of the body. Wherefore in the misery of this time this must not be esteemed the least portion, that we and other folks do daily commit grievous sins against God. Which thing thoroughly to consider maketh a good-hearted person the more desirous of death, which delivereth us from this *The griefs of all estates.* sinful life. Moreover, all conditions and estates of men have their griefs. Riches, that with great care and travail are gathered together and possessed, be sometimes lost by storm, fire, water, robbery, or theft. He that is in honour and prosperity hath enemies and evil willers. Whoso hath the governance and rule of many must also stand in fear of many things. And what occupation or handicraft can a man use, but he hath in it whereof to complain?

Not only hath a man trouble on his own behalf, but a very stony stomach and an iron heart must it be, that is not sorry when hurt doth happen to his father and mother, to his own wife, children, friends, or kinsfolk.

Furthermore, the universal trouble is manifold and piteous, specially now at this present, with noisome diseases, divisions, wars, seditions, uproars: like as one water-wave followeth upon another, and one can scarce avoid another; even so oft-times cometh one mischance in another's neck: and in this short life upon one only day to have no trouble, is a great advantage. Therefore ought we to be the less sorry, when the time of our deliverance approacheth.

Now might one object against this, and say, that this Our troubles present life hath many pleasures and pastimes withal. Never- more than theless a man must open the other eye also, and behold, that joys. in this life there is ever more sorrow than joy behind. Worldly joy is mixed, defiled, spotted, and perverted with sorrow and bitterness. It may well begin in a sorrowful matter, to bring a short fugitive pleasure; but suddenly it endeth to a man's greater heaviness. Not in vain doth the wise man say: "The Prov. xiv. heart is sorrowful even in laughter, and the end of mirth is heaviness."

Philip, the king of the Macedonians, when he upon one day had received three glad messages; one that the victory was his in the stage-play of Olympus; the second, that his captain Parmenio had with one battle overcome the Dardanes; the third, that the queen his wife was delivered of a son; he held up his hands to heaven and said: "O ye Gods, I be-seech you, that for so great and manifold prosperity ye will appoint me a competent misfortune." The wise prudent king feared the inconstancy of fortune, which, as the heathen talk thereof, envieth great prosperity. And therefore his desire was, that his exceeding welfare might be sauced with a little trouble.

Experience itself teacheth us. Where did ever one live the space of a month, or one whole day, in pleasure and ease so thoroughly, but somewhat hath offended or hindered him? Therefore earthly joy is not so great, so durable, nor so pure, but that the whole life of man may well be called a vale of misery.

CHAPTER X.

WITNESS THAT THIS LIFE IS MISERABLE.

TESTIMONY of the scripture: "Man is born to misery as Job v. the bird is to fly[1]." "The days of man are like the days of Job vii.

[1 So also Cov. Bible, following the LXX. Syr. Vulg. The autho-rised version, following, as appears, the Chaldee paraphrase and some of the Hebrew commentators: "Man is born to trouble, as the sparks fly upwards."]

an hired servant, even a breath, and nothing but vain." Look through the whole book of Ecclesiastes, the Preacher. Augustine writeth: "If a man were put to the choice, that either he must die, or else live again afresh, and suffer like things as he had suffered already before, he would rather die, specially if he thoroughly consider how many dangers and mischances he scarce yet hath escaped."

Whoso now knoweth likewise, that God through death doth make an end of misery upon earth, it bringeth him great comfort and ease. Yea, he shall rather desire death than fear it. For even holy Job himself also, when he was robbed of his health, riches, and children, and rebuked of his wife and friends, wished rather to die than to live.

1 Kings xix.   Elias, being sure in no place, desired to die. Tobias, being stricken with blindness, and misentreated of his wife, [Tobit iii.] prayed thus: " O Lord, deal with me according to thy will, and command my spirit to be received in peace; for more expedient were it for me to die than to live." If holy men now by reason of their great troubles desired death; it is no marvel if we, that are weaker and of more imperfection, be weary of this life. Yea, an unspeakable folly is it, a man to wish for to continue still in the life of misery, and not to prepare himself to another and better life.

CHAPTER XI.

THAT THE CONSIDERATION OF DEATH BEFOREHAND IS PROFITABLE TO ALL VIRTUES.

A VERY mad and unhappy man must he needs be, which thoroughly considereth, that undoubtedly he must depart hence, he knoweth not how nor when; and whether he shall then have his right mind, directing himself to God and desiring grace, he cannot tell; and will not even now out of hand begin to fear God, and serve him more diligently.

As the peacock, when he looketh upon his own feathers, is proud, but when he beholdeth his feet, letteth the feathers

42

down; even so doth man cease from pride, when he considereth his end. For in the end he shall be spoiled of all temporal beauty, strength, power, honour, and goods. " Naked Job i. came I out of my mother's womb, and naked shall I turn thither again."

Through the consideration of death may a man despise all fleshly lust and worldly joy. For even the same flesh that thou so pamperest with costly dainties and vain ornaments, must shortly be a portion for worms: neither is there a more horrible carrion than of man.

Many one through fear of death giveth alms, exerciseth charity, doth his business circumspectly. To be short; the consideration of death is even as a scourge or spur that provoketh forward, and giveth a man sufficient occasion to avoid eternal death, whereof the death of the body is a shadow. Therefore the Ninevites, fearing their own overthrow and Jonas ii. destruction, repented and fell to a perfect amendment.

CHAPTER XII.

IN DEATH WE LEARN THE RIGHT KNOWLEDGE OF OURSELVES AND OF GOD, AND ARE OCCASIONED TO GIVE OURSELVES UNTO GOD.

MANY a man in his lifetime can dissemble and shew a fair countenance; but at the point of death no hypocrisy or dissimulation hath place. There verily shall we be proved and tried, what manner of faith, love, conscience, and comfort we have, and how much we have comprehended out of the doctrine of Christ.

Then doth God let us see our own strength, how that all worldly strength is a thousand times less than we ever would have thought all the days of our life. Then perceive we seeingly and feelingly (so to say), that we stand in the only hand and power of God, and that he alone endureth still Lord and Master over death and life. Then learn we right to feel the worthiness of the passion and death of Christ, and in ourselves to have experience of the things, whereof we never took so diligent heed before in our lifetime.

Then come the fits of repentance for sins committed, that we think: " O, if I had known that God would have been so earnest, I would have left many things undone, which I (alas therefore!) have committed." Then are we forced to receive and love the gospel, which else heretofore might not come to such stout and jolly youngsters. Then begin we to run to God, to call upon him, to magnify and praise him, faithfully to cleave unto him, and uprightly to serve him.

CHAPTER XIII.

THAT THE DEAD CEASETH FROM SIN.

ALL Christians desire to be free from sin: for sin and vice doth far far vex the faithful, more than all misfortunes of the body. Now though one do keep himself from sin, yet standeth he in a slippery place; the flesh is weak, strong is the devil, of whom it is easily overcome: " Whoso standeth, let him look that he fall not."

1 Cor. x.

While the captain yet fighteth, it is uncertain whether he shall have the victory and triumph: even so, though a man do valiantly defend himself against the lusts of the flesh and temptations of the devil, he may yet fall and lose the victory. Yea, if we always lived, we should do more evil: sin ceaseth not, till we come to be blessed with a shovel. Death cutteth away sin from us, and delivereth us from unclean senses, thoughts, words, and deeds. For though death in Paradise was enjoined unto man for a penalty of sin; yet through the grace of God, in the merits of Christ, it is become unhurtful; yea, a medicine to purge out sin, and a very workhouse, wherein we are made ready to everlasting righteousness.

Like as terrible Goliath with his own sword was destroyed of David; even so with death, that came by the means of sin, is sin overcome and vanquished of Christ. If it grieved us from our hearts, that we daily see and find how we continually use ourselves against the most sweet will of our most dear Father, and were assured withal, that in death we cease

44

from sin, and begin to be perfect and righteous; how were it possible, that we should not set little by death, and patiently take it upon us? Out of such a fervent jealousy and godly displeasure Paul, after he had earnestly complained that he found another law, which strove against the law of God, sighed and cried: "Oh wretched man that I am! who shall Rom. vii. deliver me from the body of this death?" Again, so long as death hath so evil a taste in us, and we will perforce continue still in the life of the flesh; we bewray ourselves, that we do not well, nor sufficiently understand our own defaults, neither feel them deep enough, nor abhor them so much as we should; yea, that we be not earnest desirers of innocency, nor fervent lovers of our heavenly Father.

CHAPTER XIV.

THAT THE DEAD IS DELIVERED FROM THIS VICIOUS WORLD,
HAVING NOT ONLY THIS ADVANTAGE, THAT HE SINNETH
NO MORE, BUT ALSO IS DISCHARGED FROM OTHER SINS.

WHOSO leaveth nothing else worthy behind him, but that he is quiet from vicious people, may well be the gladder to depart hence; partly, for that he can be no more tempted of them, nor enticed by their evil examples; partly, for that, though he could not be deceived by others, yet it grieveth him at the heart to see other folks practise their wilfulness. Now hath vice and sin everywhere gotten the upper hand; the truth is despised, God himself dishonoured, the poor oppressed, the good persecuted, the ungodly promoted to authority, antichrist triumphing. Great complaining there is, that the world is ever the longer the worse. Forasmuch then as through death we be discharged of so vicious a world, whom should it delight to live here any more? This meaning doth the preacher set forth in the fourth chapter of Ecclesiastes, saying: "So I turned me, and considered all the violent wrong that is done under the sun. And behold, the tears of such as were oppressed, there was no man to comfort them, or that would deliver and defend them from the violence of their oppressors." There is at this day, by the grace of God, many a worthy Christian that desireth rather to die, than to be a looker upon such devilish wilfulness as commonly goeth forward.

CHAPTER XV.

THAT THE DEAD OBTAINETH SALVATION.

As for vicious unrepentant people, when they die, I know no comfort for them. Their bodies indeed shall rise at the last day, but foul and marked to eternal pain. Their souls shall be delivered unto the devil, to whom they have done service. An example hereof standeth of the rich man : again, there is the example of good Lazarus, that all Christians are taken up of the angels into eternal joy and salvation. We must not first be purged in purgatory ; but through death we escape the devil, the world, and all misfortunes that this time is oppressed withal.

Luke xvi.

If we now should lose our bodies, and not have them again, then were death indeed a terrible thing, neither precious nor much worth. But our body is not so little regarded before God : for even unto the body also hath he already prepared salvation. Yea, even for this intent hath he laid upon our necks the burden of natural death, that he might afterward clothe us with a pure, renewed, and clear body, and to make us glorious in eternal life. Therefore death also, which is a beginning of the joyful resurrection, ought to be esteemed dear and precious in our eyes. After death verily is the soul in itself cleansed from all sins, and endowed with perfect holiness, wisdom, joy, honour, and glory for evermore.

CHAPTER XVI.

SIMILITUDES THAT DEATH IS WHOLESOME.

If an old silver goblet be melted, and new-fashioned after a beautiful manner, then is it better than before, and neither

46

spilt nor destroyed. Even so have we no just cause to complain of death, whereby the body being delivered from all filthiness, shall in his due time be perfectly renewed.

The egg-shell, though it be goodly and fair-fashioned, must be opened and broken, that the young chick may slip out of it. None otherwise doth death dissolve and break up our body, but to the intent that we may attain unto the life of heaven.

The mother's womb carrieth the child seven or nine months, and prepareth it not for itself, but for the world wherein we are born. Even so this present time over all upon earth serveth not to this end, that we must ever be here, but that we should be brought forth and born out of the body of the world into another and everlasting life. Hereunto behold the words of Christ: " A woman, when she travaileth, hath sorrow because her hour is come: but as soon as she is delivered of the child, she remembereth no more the anguish, for joy that a man is born into the world." Namely, like as a child out of the small habitation of his mother's womb, with danger and anguish is born into this wide world; even so goeth a man through the narrow gate of death with distress and trouble, out of the earth into the heavenly life. *John xvi.*

For this cause did the old Christians call the death of the saints a new birth. Therefore ought we to note well this comfort, that to die is not to perish, but to be first of all born aright.

The death of the faithful seemeth indeed to be like unto the death of the unbelievers: but verily this is as great a difference as between heaven and earth. Our death is even as a death-image made of wood, which grinneth with the teeth, and feareth, but cannot devour. Our death should be esteemed even as Moses' brasen serpent; which, having the form and proportion of a serpent, was yet without biting, without moving, without poisoning. Even so, though death be not utterly taken away, yet through the grace of God it is so weakened and made void, that the only bare proportion remaineth. When the master of the ship thinketh he is not wide from the place where he must land and discharge, he saileth on forth the more cheerfully and gladly: even so, the nearer we draw unto death, where we must land, the more stoutly ought we to fight against the ghostly perils. Like as he that goeth a far journey hath uncertain lodging, travail, and labour, and desireth to return home to his own country, to his father and mother, wife, children and friends, among whom he is surest, and at most quiet; by means whereof he forceth[1] the less for any rough careful path or way homeward: even so all we are strangers and pilgrims upon earth. Our home is paradise in heaven; our heavenly father is God, the earthly father of all men is Adam; our spiritual fathers are the patriarchs, prophets, and apostles, which altogether wait and long for us. Seeing now that death is the path and way unto them, we ought the less to fly it, to the intent that we may come to our right home, salute our fathers and friends, embrace them, and dwell with them for ever. We have here no remaining city, but we seek one to come. Our conversation and burghership is in heaven.

But if any man be afraid of death, and force not for the country of heaven, only because of temporal pleasures, the same dealeth unhonestly; even as do they, that whereas they ought to go the next way home, set them down in a pleasant place, or among companions at the tavern: where they lying still, forget their own country, and pass not upon their friends and kinsfolks. How evil this becometh them, every man may well consider by himself.

The Lord Jesus giveth this similitude: " Except the wheat corn fall into the ground and die, it bideth alone: but if it die, it bringeth forth much fruit." Likewise Paul compareth us men unto grains of corn, the churchyard to a field. To die, he saith, is to be sown upon God's field. The resurrection, with the life that followeth after, resembleth he to the pleasant green corn in summer.

If a man lie in a dark miserable prison, with this condition that he should not come forth, till the walls of the tower were fallen down, undoubtedly he would be right glad to see the walls begin to fall: our soul is kept in within the body upon earth, as in captivity and bonds. Now as soon as the body is at a point that it must needs fall, why would we be sorry? For by this approacheth the deliverance, when we out of the prison of misery shall be brought before the most amiable countenance of God, into the joyful freedom of heaven. Ac-

1 Chron. xxix.
Psal. xxxix.
cxix.
1 Pet. ii.
2 Cor. v.
Phil. iii.
Heb. xi. xiii.
1 Cor. xv.

Heb. xiii.
Phil. iii.

1 Cor. xv.

[1 To force: to lay stress upon. Johnson.]

48

cording to this did David pray: "Bring my soul out of Psal. cxlii. prison, O Lord, that I may give thanks unto thy name." Item, in many places of scripture, *to die* is called *to sleep;* death itself, a sleep. Like as it is no grief for a man to go to sleep, nor when he seeth his parents and friends lay them down to rest; (for he knoweth that such as are asleep do soon awake and rise again;) so when we or our friends depart 1 Cor. xv. away by death, we ought to erect and comfort ourselves with 1 Thess. iv. the resurrection.

CHAPTER XVII.

WITNESS THAT DEATH IS WHOLESOME.

For the strengthening of our faith, I will allege evident testimony of God's word. The preacher saith: "The day Eccl. vii. of death is better than the day of birth." As if he would say: In the day of thy birth thou art sent into the cold, into the heat, into hunger and thirst, wherein is sin and wretchedness: in the day of thy death thou shalt be delivered from all evil. Again we read: "Though the righteous Wisd. iv. be overtaken with death, yet shall he be in rest."

"Verily, verily, I say unto you, he that heareth my John v. words, and believeth on him that sent me, hath everlasting life, and shall not come into damnation, but is escaped from death into life." "If we live, we live unto the Lord: if we Rom. xiv. die, we die unto the Lord. Therefore whether we live or die, 2 Cor. iv. we are the Lord's." Behold, how comfortably this is spoken of all Christians.

CHAPTER XVIII.

THAT DEATH CANNOT BE AVOIDED. ITEM, OF COMPANIONS OF THEM THAT DIE.

Upon this condition are we born into the world, into this light, not to continue alway therein; but when God will, through temporal death to lay aside and put off the travail of this miserable life. Witty men have found out, how hard stones may be broken and mollified, and how wild beasts may be tamed : but nothing could they invent, whereby death might be avoided. It is not unwisely said : " God's hand may a man escape, but not death."

Metrodorus writeth, that against bodily enemies there may be made fortresses, castles, and bulwarks ; but so far as concerneth death, all men have an unfenced city. In other dangers, power, money, flight, counsel, and policy may help : but as for death, it can neither be banished with power, nor bought with money, nor avoided with flying away, nor prevented with counsel, nor turned back with policy. And though thou be now delivered from sickness, yet within a little while thou must, whether thou wilt or no, depart hence to death's home ; for the highest lawgiver of all told our first

Gen. ii.

father so before : " In what day soever thou eatest thereof, thou shalt die the death." Understand, that the death of the soul bringeth with it the death of the body.

Whoso now grudgeth, and is not content to die, what is that else, but that he, forgetting himself and his own nature, complaineth of God in heaven, that he suffered him to be born, and made him not an angel ?

Why should we refuse the thing that we have common with other men ? Now doth death touch not only us, but high and low estate, young and old, man and woman, master and servant.

As many as came of the first man must lay down their necks. Death is an indifferent judge, regardeth no person, hath no pity on the fatherless, careth not for the poor, dispenseth not with the rich, feareth not the mighty, passeth not for the noble, honoureth not the aged, spareth not the wise, pardoneth not the foolish.

For like as a river is poisoned in the well-spring, or fountain, so was the nature of man altogether in our first parents. And forasmuch as they themselves were maimed through sin, they have begotten unright and mortal children.

Rom. v.

Touching this saith Paul: " By one man came death upon all men."

Now let us consider, what excellent companions and holy fellowship they also have that are dead. Paul writeth, that " we must be like shapen unto the image of the Son of God."

If he now that of nature was immortal and innocent, became mortal for our sakes, even Jesus Christ our Saviour; why would we then, that many and sundry ways have deserved death, continue here still, and not die? Abraham the faithful, Sampson the strong, Solomon the wise, Absolom the fair one, yea, all the prophets and apostles, kings and emperors, through death departed out of this life. A very dainty and tender body must that be, which, considering so great multitudes of corpses, doth yet out of measure vex himself, because the like shall happen unto him. That were even like as if one would take upon himself to be better than all righteous and holy men, that ever were since the beginning of the world.

CHAPTER XIX.

OF NATURAL HELP IN DANGER OF DEATH.

Whoso will help himself from the pestilence with flying away, leaving his own wife, friends, and neighbours; he declareth unperfectness of faith, and standeth not with christian charity, where we owe unto others the same that we in like case would gladly have at their hands.

Grant that the pestilence is such an infectious sickness, as one taketh of another. What then? If one stand in battle array to fight for his country, must not he also look for a gun-stone to be sent him into his bosom to carry home? doth it therefore beseem him to break the array and to fly? Like as there the enemies of the body are at hand; so here do the ghostly adversaries besiege the soul of him that is a dying, where one Christian should help another with worthy talk. Therefore is that a foolish unadvised counsel, when we with neglecting of our own members will flee from the wrath of God, thinking through sin to escape the punishment of sin. Experience also doth shew, that such folks do oft perish, as well as other; yea, sooner than they that fled not at all. But physic is permitted of God, as in the time of pestilence with fires and perfumes to make the air more wholesome from poison, and to receive somewhat into the body, for the consuming of evil humours, and to hinder the infection. Item, when one is taken with a disease, to be let blood, to sweat, to follow the physician's instruction; such things are in no wise to be reprehended, so that, whether it turn to death or life, the heart only and hope hang upon God. The physician should neither be despised nor worshipped. For to think scorn to use medicine in sickness, what were that else but even to tempt God?

CHAPTER XX.

THAT GOD IS ABLE AND WILL HELP FOR CHRIST'S SAKE.

SPECIALLY when death is at hand, a man findeth no help in any creature of heaven and earth, whereby he might fortunately suppress the exceeding great fear of death, but only in God the Father, in Christ his Son, and in the Holy Spirit of them both.

It is God that knoweth the perils of thy death, and can meddle withal. Through his power shalt thou get through, and drink the bitter draught. Though we die, yet liveth God before us, with us, after us, and is able to preserve us for ever. Christ sayeth: "Weep not, the damsel is not dead, but sleepeth." Faithless reason understandeth not the mystery of God, and laugheth: but Christ, the true God, hath both the word and work together, and saith no more but "Arise;" and the soul came again to the body, and she arose. Out of this, and such like examples, oughtest thou, faint-hearted man, to understand the infinite power of God, who can receive thy soul also and preserve it.

Not only is God able, but will also help graciously. Why should not he lay upon thee some great thing, as death is, seeing he addeth so great advantage, help, and strength thereto, to prove what his grace and power may do? For he hath numbered all the hairs of our head: that is, he alway hath his eyes upon us, and careth ever for us.

Yea, that he loveth us more than we love ourselves, and maketh better provision for us than we can wish, he hath openly and evidently testified in his own dear Son; whom he caused to take our miserable nature upon him, and therein for the sins of all the world to suffer, to die, to rise again, to ascend up to heaven, where he sitteth at the right hand of

Matt. x. Luke xii. Psal. xxxiv. Psal. lx. 1 Pet. v.

Mark xvi. Luke xxii. Acts vii. Rom. viii. Eph. i. iv. Philip. ii.

God the Father Almighty. Among the which articles, every Col. iii. one doth help and comfort such as are a dying. 1 Pet. iii. Heb. i. ii. x. xii.

The natural Son of God himself from heaven became a Psal. cx. The mortal man, to the intent that man's mortal nature, through humanity of Christ. the uniting thereof with the immortal nature of the Godhead in his own only person, might be exalted to an immortal life.

He, having a natural fear of death, said: "My soul is The passion of Christ. heavy, even unto death." He prayed also: "Father, if it be Matt. xxvi. possible, take this cup from me." But this fear and terror John xii. did he overcome; for he added thereto and saith: "Father, Luke xxii. not my will, but thine be fulfilled." Through this victory of Christ, may all Christians also overcome such terror and fear as they be in.

Item, though the Jews blaspheme never so much, and say, "Let him come down from the cross: he hath helped other, let him now help himself;" as though they would say, "There, there, seest thou death, like a wretch must thou die," and no man is able to help thee; yet did the Lord Jesus hold his peace there-to, as if he heard and saw them not. He made no answer again, but only regarded the good will and pleasure of his Father. Therefore though we have an horrible temptation of death, as though there were neither comfort nor help for us any more, yet in Christ and with Christ we may endure all, and wait still upon the gracious good will of God. He did not only suffer the horror and temptation of death, but death itself; yea, the most horrible death, whereby he took from us the death eternal, and some deal mollified and assuaged our temporal death: yea, besides this, he made it profitable and wholesome; so that death, which of itself should else be a beginning of everlasting sorrow, is become an entrance into eternal salvation. According to this meaning are the words of Paul, when he saith, that "Christ, by the grace of God, tasted death for all men." 2 Cor. v. Phil. i. Rom. vii.

Item, "He became partaker of flesh and blood, to put Heb. ii. down through death him that had the lordship over death, that is to say, the devil; and that he might deliver them, which through fear of death, were all their life-time in danger of bondage."

Moreover, that Christ is the living and immortal image against death, yea, the very power of our resurrection and of life everlasting, he himself hath testified with his own joy- Christ's resurrection.

53

ful and victorious resurrection; and also with that, that in
Matt. xxvii. his resurrection many other saints that were dead rose from
death again.

Again, how full is it of comfort and pure treasure, that
St Paul joineth our resurrection unseparably to the resurrection of Jesus Christ! Likewise doth St Paul comfort his
2 Tim. ii.
Rom. vi. disciple Timothy with the resurrection, and saith: " If we
die with Christ, we shall live with him; if we be patient, we
shall also reign with him."

No less must the fruit of the ascension of Christ be considered. For the Son of God hath promised and said:
[John xvii.] " Father I will, that where I am, they also be whom thou
hast given me." Seeing that Christ now with body and soul
is gone up to heaven, what can be thought more comfortable
for a man at his death, than that we Christians shall also
after death be taken up into the joy of heaven ?

In heaven sitteth Christ at the right hand of God, Lord
and King over sin, devil, death, and hell. Him we have in
that heavenly life with God an assured faithful mediator and
helper. Though we must fight in extremity of death, yet
are we not alone in this conflict or battle; even the valiant
heavenly captain himself, who upon the cross overcame death
and all misfortune for our sakes, hath respect unto us from
Deut. i. xx.
Exod. xiv.
Jos. xxiii.
1 Chron. vi.
2 Chron. xx.
xxxii.
2 Kings vi.
Zech. x. time to time, goeth before us in our battle, and fighteth for
us, keepeth us from all mischances in the way to salvation;
so that we need not care nor fear, that we shall sink or fall
down to the bottom.

He shall cause us with our own bodily eyes to see the
glorious victory and triumph in the resurrection of the dead,
and to have experience thereof in our own body and soul.
Death is even as a dark cave in the ground: but whoso
taketh Christ's light candle, putteth his trust in him, and
goeth into the dim dark hole, the mist flieth before him, and
the darkness vanisheth away.

In Christ have we a mighty effectuous image of grace, of
life, and of salvation, in such sort, that we Christians should
fear neither death nor other misfortune. Summa, he is our
hope, our safeguard, our triumph, our crown.

John xi. Witness of scripture: " I am the resurrection and the
life: he that believeth on me, yea, though he were dead, yet
shall he live; and whosoever liveth and believeth in me shall

never die." Forthwith, after he had spoken these words, raised he up Lazarus, who had lain four days in the grave, and began to corrupt and stink.

"As by Adam all die, so by Christ shall all be made 1 Cor. xv. alive, every one in his order." Item, "Our burghership is in Phil. iii. heaven: from whence we look for a Saviour, even Jesus Christ; which shall change our vile bodies, that they may be fashioned like unto his glorious body, according to the working whereby he is able to subdue all things unto himself." Also: "Ye are dead, and your life is hid with Christ Col. iii. in God. But when Christ your life shall shew himself, then shall ye also appear with him in glory." Here doth Paul declare, that our life is not in this world, but hid with Christ in God, and shall through Christ in his time be gloriously opened. After this manner should Christ be printed into the feeble, troubled, and doubtful consciences of the sick. And with all diligence ought the office of Christ to be considered, how that he, according unto the scripture, coming into this world for our wealth, did also for our wealth preach, wrought miracles, suffered, and died, to deliver us out of this false unhappy world, to open unto us the right door into eternal life, and to bring us with body and soul into heaven; wherein neither sin, death, nor devil shall be able to hinder us for evermore.

Who shall ever be able sufficiently to praise and magnify the infinite glory of the grace of God? What would we have the Lord our God to do more for us, to make us lustily step forth before the face of death, manfully to fight in all trouble, and willingly to wait for the deliverance?

CHAPTER XXI.

THAT GOD HATH PROMISED HIS HELP AND COMFORT.

Out of this exceeding grace of God, for the blessed Seed's sake, proceed God's comfortable promises in the old and new Testament. "Mine eyes shall still be upon thee, that Psal. xci. thou perish not. The Lord shall deliver thee from the snare of the hunter, and from the most noisome death. With his own wings shall he cover thee; so that under his feathers thou shalt be safe. His truth and faithfulness shall be thy shield and buckler : so that thou shalt neither need to fear any inconvenience by night, neither swift arrow in the day-season; neither the pestilence that creepeth in darkness, nor yet any hurt that destroyeth by day-time. Though a thousand fall on thy left hand, and ten thousand on thy right, yet shall it not touch thee."

Here doth God evidently promise, that he will graciously preserve his own children, first, from such temptation, phantasy, and deceivableness, as come upon a man by night in the dark: secondly, from the violence of wicked unthrifts, and all mischances that overtake men openly in the day-season, yea, sometimes suddenly and unawares : thirdly, from the pestilence, that we need not to fear it, though there die of it a thousand on the left hand and ten thousand on the right : the pestilence shall either not take us, or not wound us unto death, or else serve to our everlasting welfare: fourthly, from hot feverish sicknesses, such as commonly grow in hot countries, when the sun shineth most strongly. Under these four plagues are all mischances comprehended.

In the end of this psalm stand these words : "I am with him in trouble, I will deliver him, and bring him to honour." When God saith, "I am with him," consider not thou thine own powers; for they help nothing at all : behold much more the power of him that is with thee in trouble. When thou hearest, "I will deliver him," thou must not be faint-hearted, though the trouble do seem long to continue. When thou hearest, "I will bring him unto honour," be thou sure, that as thou art partaker of the death of Christ, so shalt thou be also of his glory.

Matt. xi.

Christ calleth thee to him, and crieth yet still : "Come to me, all ye that labour and are laden, and I will ease you. Take my yoke on you, and learn of me, that I am meek and lowly in heart, and ye shall find rest unto your souls." Again:

[John viii.]

"Verily, verily, I say unto you; If any man keep my sayings, he shall never see death." Understand, that the light of life doth shine clearer, than the darkness of death can blind. For the faithful, through his belief, is after such sort incorporated and joined unto the Lord Christ, the true life, that he shall not be separated from him. Though body and

56

soul depart asunder now for a season; yet is that done in an assured undoubted hope of the blessed resurrection, that very shortly both body and soul shall come together again to eternal joy. And thus the christian believer neither seeth, feeleth, nor tasteth the everlasting death of his body and soul, that is to say, eternal damnation.

CHAPTER XXII.

GOD SETTETH TO HIS OWN HELPING HAND IN SUCH WISE AND AT SUCH TIME AS IS BEST OF ALL.

GOD now, through Christ, doth not only promise most graciously his comfort and help, but faithfully performeth he the same in due season, so far, and after such sort as is expedient. The very right time undoubtedly doth not he omit. Death indeed is a narrow way; but God shorteneth it. The bitterness of death passeth all the pains that we have felt upon earth; but it endureth not long. Death must make quick speed with us, as Hezekiah the king of Judah saith: "He shall cut off my life, as a weaver doth his web." And Isai. xxxviii. when the pain is greatest of all, then is it near the end. Hereunto may be applied that Christ said, "It is but a John xiv. modicum, a very little while." Though it were so that the troubles of death did long endure, yet towards the eternity that followeth after is the same scarce as one point or prick in comparison of a whole circle. In the mean season, God can more comfort and help, than the most horrible death of all is able to disturb or grieve. Sometime taketh he from us the grievous enemy or mortal sickness, and so delivereth us out of the perils of death. Else giveth he some ease or refreshing outwardly: or if the trouble go on still, he sendeth his sweet gracious comfort inwardly, so as the patient through the working of the Holy Ghost doth feel a taste, a proof and beginning of the heavenly joy; by means whereof he is able willingly to forsake all that earthly is, and to endure all manner of pain and smart until the end.

"The Spirit of God certifieth our spirit, that we are the Rom. viii.

children of God. If we be children, we are also heirs, the heirs, I mean, of God, and heirs annexed with Christ, if so be that we suffer with him, that we may also be glorified with him." God commandeth his angels, that they with him do look unto thee, O man, when thou diest, and to take heed unto thy soul, to keep it, and to receive it, when it shall Psal. xxxiv. depart out of the body. Witness this is : " The angel of the Lord pitcheth round about them that fear him, and delivereth Psal. xci. them." And : " He hath given his angels charge concerning thee, that they keep thee in all thy ways, and bear thee in their hands, that thou hurt not thy foot against a stone."

Heb. i.   The angels, which are many without number, be ministering spirits, sent to do service for their sakes, which shall be heirs of salvation. Therefore a Christian at his last end must be thoroughly assured, that in his death he is not alone, but that very many eyes look unto him : first, the eyes of God the Father himself, and of his Son Jesus Christ; then the worthy angels, and all Christians upon earth.

Then, according to the contents of the sacrament of baptism and of the supper of the Lord, all Christians, as a whole body to a member thereof, resort unto him that is a dying, by having compassion and prayer to help him by, that at his death he may overcome death, sin, and hell.

CHAPTER XXIII.

EXAMPLES OF GOD'S HELP.

In the time of the prophets and apostles God raised certain from death ; to the intent that our weak feeble nature might have the more help to believe the resurrection and eternal life. For the dead could not have been raised, if death did bring man utterly to nought. Abraham fell sick, and died in a good age, when he was old, and had lived enough, and was put unto his people ; that is, his soul came to the soul of the other saints, which died before. So is it Gen. xxxv. also of Isaac. Word was brought to king Hezekiah, that he should live no longer ; but after he had made his earnest prayer unto God, there were added fifteen years unto life.

When Lazarus died, his soul was carried of the angels into Luke xvi. Abraham's bosom. The murderer upon the cross heard in his extreme trouble that Christ said unto him : " This day Luke xxiii. shalt thou be with me in paradise."

Daily experience testifieth, that God forsaketh ˙not his own. Therefore undoubtedly he that hath begun his king-dom in us, shall graciously perform and finish it.

CHAPTER XXIV.

THAT IT IS NECESSARY TO PREPARE FOR THIS JOURNEY.

If we could find in our hearts gladly for to hear, how unhurtful, yea, wholesome and vincible death is become through Christ, we would not be idle, and linger still till the time came that we must needs die.

A good householder maketh provision for himself and his family, and buyeth beforehand fuel and victuals, and such things as he hath need of for a whole year, or for a month, &c., according as he is able. Much more ought a Christian to provide that, which concerneth not only one month or one year, but an eternity that hath no end. Like as faithful servants wait for their master, so ought we to look for the coming of Christ, when he shall call us out of this time. " If Luke xii. the householder knew what hour the thief would come, he would watch, and not suffer his house to be broken up. Therefore be ye also ready : for in the hour that ye think Matt. xxiv not, will the Son of man come."

Whoso hath perfect knowledge of death, as it is hitherto described and set forth, he in making provision beforehand hath first this advantage, that it is good fighting with a known enemy. Contrariwise, on the other side, what shall an unmeet warrior do, that knoweth not the nature, subtlety, weapons, and policy of the enemy ?

CHAPTER XXV.

PROVISION CONCERNING TEMPORAL GOODS, CHILDREN, AND FRIENDS, WHICH MUST BE LEFT BEHIND.

AGAIN, concerning temporal goods: Let the rich who hath wife and children, or other heirs, make provision for them in good order under writing, according as in every place the custom is. But if honour and authority, substance or goods, go too near thy stomach, then consider that they be not true, but uncertain, transitory, and vain goods, which bring more unquietness than rest. Consider also, that many more rich mighty princes, kings, and lords must be spoiled of all their glory, and be fain to content themselves with a short narrow place of the grave.

Though we here lose all, yet do we scarce lose one farthing. And in the other life we have not kingdoms, nor empires, but God himself and everlasting goods; in comparison whereof, all minstrelsy, pastime, pomp, mirth, and cheer upon earth is scarce to be esteemed as casting counters towards the finest coins of gold. Therefore ought we to learn, specially in sickness, to give all temporal goods their leave, and to bid them farewell: And if any man will furthermore disquiet and trouble us in telling us still of them, then must we require him to depart and let us alone. Whoso hath a train hanging upon him, as father, mother, sisters, brothers, wife, children, and friends, the same is the sorer laid at: for naturally we all are loth to depart from them. Here must

Matt. x.

we remember the words of Christ: "He that loveth father or mother more than me, is not worthy of me. And he that loveth son or daughter more than me, is not meet for me. And whoso taketh not up his cross and followeth me, is unapt for me." Therefore must thou break thine own will, take up thy cross, and give over thyself unto the will of God; specially, forasmuch as even they whom thou art loth to leave behind thee upon earth, shall shortly come to thee. And in the mean season, when thou departest from thy friends, thou goest the next way, and speedest thee unto better and more loving friends. And therefore the holy patriarch Jacob said,

Gen. xlix.

when he should die: "I shall be gathered unto my people."

Item, unto Moses and Aaron said God: "Thou shalt go to [Numb. xxvii. xx.] thy people and unto thy fathers." Hereby is it declared, that death is a passage to many more folks and better friends than we leave here. There is God our Father, his Son our Brother, his heaven our inheritance, and all angels and saints our brethren, sisters, and kinsfolks, with whom we shall enjoy eternal goods for ever.

Again, whoso leaveth behind him a poor wife, children not brought up, and friends that are in necessity, must also do his best, committing them to the protection, help, and comfort of God, with an earnest prayer that he will graciously take the governance of them. For our wives, children, and posterity doth the second commandment set in God's tuition, when it saith: "Mercy and kindness shew I unto [Exod. xx.] thousands of them that love me, and keep my commandments."

Item, God writeth himself a father of the widows and [Exod. xxii. Psal. cxlv.] fatherless, and taketh them into his own protection.

Now if thou receive not this godly consolation and comfort, then, to thine own great notable hurt, thou disquietest thyself so grievously, that thou canst consider nothing that is right and just, eternal or heavenly.

CHAPTER XXVI.

PREPARATION CONCERNING GHOSTLY MATTERS, WITH WHAT COGITATIONS THE MIND OUGHT MOST TO BE EXERCISED.

MOREOVER, the sick must give all other worldly matters their leave, that the soul be not tangled with any earthly business, but directed upward into heaven, where it desireth everlastingly to live.

Here shall it be needful, that our mind have an assured understanding of the holy gospel. In this consideration endure thou still; hang thou thereupon with stedfast faith, whereout grow these fruits, prayer, righteousness, patience, and all goodness.

After the doctrine of the true gospel, without thine own

and religious men's works, without the merits of saints, art thou justified, made righteous, and saved only through Christ, who alone is thy mediator, advocate, helper, satisfaction, hope, comfort, and life. It is Christ's will to convey thee away from sin, from the world, from the devil, and from hell, and to take thee to his grace into the eternal paradise, though all creatures were against thee.

John xvii.   Probation out of the scripture: "This is the life eternal, that they know thee to be the only true God, and whom thou hast sent, Jesus Christ." With this evangelical doctrine, and with nothing else, must our hearts be occupied, what temptations soever happen, which undoubtedly will not tarry behind.

While we go about yet merry and in health, it bringeth exceeding great profit, if we exercise ourselves with the cogitations of death. But in sickness, and when we must die, that is, when the horrible image of death would make us afraid, we must not unquiet ourselves with heavy remembrance of death. We should not behold or consider death in itself, nor in our own nature, neither in them that are slain through the wrath of God; but principally in Christ Jesu, and then in his saints, which through him overcame death, and died in the grace of God. From this fight may not we suffer ourselves to be driven, though all angels and all creatures, yea, though God himself, in our opinion, would lay other things before our eyes, which they do not: howbeit, the evil spirit maketh such an appearance. For Christ Jesus is nothing else but life and salvation. Yea, the more deeply and stedfastly we do set, print, and behold Christ before us, the more shall death be despised and devoured in life; the heart also hath the more rest, and may quietly die in Christ.

John xvi.   Therefore saith Christ: "In the world, that is, also, in yourselves, ye shall have trouble; but in me peace. Be ye of good comfort, I have overcome the world."

Rev. xiv.
Numb. xxi.   "Blessed are they that die in the Lord." This aforetime was figured and signified, when the children of Israel, being bitten of fiery serpents, might not struggle with them, but behold the brasen serpent, namely Christ. So the quick serpents fell away of themselves, and vanished.

When we now behold death and the pangs of death in itself with our own feeble reason, without Christ, without

God's word, specially out of season, that is to say, in the danger of death; then hath death his whole power and strength in our feeble nature, and killeth us with the greater pain, so that we forget God, and are lost for ever.

CHAPTER XXVII.

OF REPENTANCE AND SORROW FOR SIN.

To the intent that our will, heart, and mind may right and truly receive and apprehend the Lord Christ, we must first be thoroughly sorrowful for our sinful life, and confess that there was no remedy, but of ourselves we should have been damned for ever. This shrift or confession of sins must not forthwith be done to the priest, but unto God, with hearty sorrow and repentance, after the example of the poor sinner and of the publican. Therefore must we also acknowledge, that with all our own power and works we are able to prevail neither against death, nor other mischance. For how were it possible, that we, poor silly worms, feeble and weak in body and soul, should be able to endure the stormy waves and intolerable burden of death, if the right hand of God himself were not present to help our infirmity? Full truly spake a certain king in France, when he lay on his death-bed: "I have been very rich, I have had exceeding much honour, my power was passing great; and yet for all my riches, power, and friends, I am not able to obtain of death so much as one hour's respite."

CHAPTER XXVIII.

OF TRUE FAITH.

To such a confession belongeth the christian belief, that we turn ourselves away from all comfort of man, yea, from all creatures, to the only Creator through Jesus Christ, and to give ourselves over wholly unto him. With all our natural reason and wisdom shall we never be able to comprehend, how it cometh to pass, that the soul must depart out, and yet be preserved; that worms consume the body, and that the same yet shall rise again and live for ever. Therefore is there required faith in Christ and in his word. The sum hereof have we in the twelve articles of the old ancient undoubted christian belief.

And though it be our duty alway, specially at the time of death, earnestly to consider all the articles, yet principally, when we die, we ought to exercise the four last articles; "the communion of saints, the forgiveness of sins, the resurrection of the body, and the life everlasting." For these four in themselves comprehend all the power, commodity, and fruit of faith: namely, whosoever doth stedfastly look for all grace and help at God's hand through the conception and birth, death and passion, resurrection and ascension, intercession and merits of Jesus Christ, and standeth, liveth, and dieth in the same faith; though all sins, devils, death, and hell would fall upon him and oppress him, yet can they not hurt him.

The fruits of faith.

To be short, it is not otherwise possible: he must needs have fellowship with God and the elect, and be quite discharged from all sins, and joyfully rise again to eternal life. Yea, whatsoever the Son of God himself hath, can do, and is able, that same hath this believer also obtained; neither can it go otherwise with him but prosperously in life and death, here and in the world to come, temporally and eternally.

Witness: whoso hath Christ, hath already the true life and all blessing; for Christ is the life, the resurrection, and a plentiful sufficiency of all good things. Through faith doth Christ dwell in our hearts. Therefore through faith we obtain all consolation and blessing.

Eph. iii.

That faith is the true absolution, it may be perceived by the words of Christ, when he saith so oft in the gospel: "Be it unto thee according to thy belief."

Item, God will constantly stand to his word and promise; he is of nature the truth itself. Heaven and earth shall pass, but his words shall not pass.

Luke xxi.

What are now the promises of God? "So God loved the world, that he gave his only-begotten Son, that whosoever believeth on him, should not perish, but have everlasting life." O how blessed a promise is this, that if we believe in Christ the Son of God, we shall through him inherit eternal life!

John iii.

Item: "Verily, verily, I say unto you, he that heareth my words, and believeth on him that sent me, hath everlasting life, and shall not come into damnation, but is escaped from death unto life." Lord, how comfortable a thing is this, that a faithful believer by temporal death escapeth through, yea, is already escaped into everlasting life!

Again: "This is the will of my Father, which hath sent John vi. me, that every one which seeth the Son and believeth on him, have eternal life; and I shall raise him up at the last day." As though he said: "This is the most gentle good-will of God the Father, and of God the Son, that such a man as still endureth in stedfast confidence upon the grace and word of God, shall be preserved and saved for ever. And even as little shall sin, hell, and the devil be able to hurt him, as they could hurt Christ himself. When the darkness of the A pithy similitude. night falleth down, it covereth the whole world, dimmeth the colour and fashion of all creatures, feareth and discomforteth them; yet is it not of such power, as to darken, suppress, and quench the least light of all that is found in the world. For the darker the night is, the clearer do the stars shine; yea, the least light of a candle withstandeth the whole night, and giveth light round about in the midst of darkness. A little spark also of a coal cannot the darkness cover, much less is it able to quench it. Now is God the true, everlasting, 1 John i. and heavenly light. And all they that put their trust in him are as a burning candle. For through faith doth God dwell in our hearts, and we are the living temple of God, and Christ's disciples are called the lights of the world. Hereout followeth it, that though the prince of spiritual darkness thrust in with his noisome poison and plagues; yet shall we behold in faith, that he with his poison and plagues can neither apprehend nor destroy any true faithful man or woman, but shall be smitten back and driven away perforce.

A little vein of water breaketh forth out of the ground An apt similitude. sometime scarce a finger big; and when the water is gathered into a ditch or pond, it springeth nevertheless. And though the water become heavy of certain hundred weight, and move about the fountain, yet can it not drive back the fountain, but it driveth the whole weight of the water backward and forward, and springeth still continually, till the ditch be so full that it go over. And if the other water be foul and troubled, it cannot mingle itself among the fresh clear water of the fountain; but the same remaineth pure and fair, till in time it come far from the head spring.

Jer. ii.
Psal. xxxvi.
John vii.
Now is God the only plentiful fountain of all life. And the faithful are very flowing wells. For Christ saith: "Whoso believeth on me, out of his body, as saith the scripture, shall flow streams of the water of life." Which words "he spake of the Spirit, that they which believe on him should receive." Thus no mischance of this world can spoil any faithful man of his comfort and life; forasmuch as God, the eternal well-spring of life, dwelleth and floweth in his heart, and driveth all noisome things far away from it.

The exercise of faith.
To the intent now that thou mayest be partaker of all the fruits of faith, thou must manfully strive and exercise thy belief after this manner. If any imagination or thought concerning sin or death will fear thee, though flesh and blood tell thee otherwise, and though thine own natural reason would make thee to believe none other, and thou thyself feelest not the contrary, but that God of very wrath will kill thee and damn thee for ever; yet let no despair pluck the noble comfort of the Saviour out of thine heart; let not thy heart waver in the loving and fatherly promises of God; let the terrible cogitations pass, as much as is possible. Remember
Blessed of God is he that hath this mind.
the comfortable gracious word of the Lord Jesu. Comprehend and keep it sure in a stedfast belief, confidence, and hope. Pluck up thine heart, and say: O death, thy false fear would fain deceive me, and with lying cogitations pull me away from Christ, the worthy. I may not hearken to thy fear, neither accept it. I know of a dear, valiant, worthy, and victorious man, that said: "Be of good comfort, I have overcome the world;" that is to say, sin, death, devil, hell, and
John vi.
whatsoever cleaveth to the world; and, "Verily, verily, he that believeth and putteth his trust in me, hath eternal life." With the which words the same dear, valiant, worthy, and victorious man doth apply also unto me his victory and power. With him will I continue, and keep me to his word and comfort, whether I live longer, or must die. Here ought we perfectly to be sure, that the greater the battle of death is, the nearer is Jesus Christ, to crown us with mercy and loving-kindness.

Evident examples out of the new and old Testament.

Paul rejoiceth, and boasteth against the terror of death: "Death is swallowed up in victory. Death, where is thy victory? Hell, where is thy sting?" As though he would say: O death, thou mayest well make one afraid, as a death-image of wood may do; but to devour thou hast no might. For thy victory, sting, and power is swallowed up in the victory of Christ. And through Jesus Christ our Lord hath God given us the victory against thee, so that all true faithful Christians are become lords over death and hell. But of such a faith is Paul not afraid to say: "Whether we live or die, we are the Lord's." *1 Cor. xv.* *To the faithful death is a comfort.* *Rom. xiv.*

And again thus he speaketh exceeding comfortably: "Christ is to me life, and death is to me advantage." For hereby go we from labour to rest, from shame to honour, from heaviness to joy, from death to life. "We know that we are translated from death unto life." "Though I walk in the valley of the shadow of death, yet fear I no evil; for thou, Lord, art with me." *Phil. i.* *Oh that these words were printed in our hearts. 1 John v.* *Psal. xxiii.*

Therefore let them fear death, that know not Christ, neither believe in him; even such as from temporal death pass unto death everlasting. For God giveth charge and commandment, that we should receive comfort in the Lord Jesu, as the words sound: "Be of good comfort, I have overcome the world." Whoso now will not be comforted with the Lord Jesu, doth unto God the Father and the Son the greatest dishonour; as though it were false that he biddeth us, "Be of a good comfort;" and as though it were not true, that he "hath overcome the world." And by this, whereas the devil, sin, and death is overcome already, we strengthen them to be our own tyrants against the faithful true Saviour. Hereof proceed such words as these: "I wot not how to endure and abide it: alas! what shall become of me?" What is that else, but to have respect unto our own strength, as though Christ were not at hand to take our part, and to finish the matter? Item, through unbelief a man desireth to remain here longer, whether God be content withal, or no. In the sight of the world he is taken to be no honest man, that vilely forsaketh his bodily master: doth not he then procure unto himself everlasting shame, that in trouble of death picketh himself away from Christ, the heavenly master? Witness: "He that be- *Unbelief.* *How God is blasphemed by our fear of death.* *The fearer of death armeth the devil against himself.* *Trust in our own strength is the way to desperation.* *Mark xvi.*

John iii. lieveth not shall be damned. He that believeth not on the Son of God, shall not see life, but the wrath of God abideth on him."

CHAPTER XXIX.

OF HOPE.

The work and strength of the lively faith.

FAITH, though it be no greater than a little spark, gendereth hope, which looketh and waiteth for the deliverance
Psal. xxxvii. to come, and shall undoubtedly not come to confusion. "Commit thy cause unto the Lord, hope upon him; and he full well shall bring it to pass." *Ipse faciet*, he himself will be the doer.

The good patriarch Abraham is set forth unto us for an example of faith and hope. Like as he hoped against hope, that is to say, there as nothing was to hope; even so must our hope stand fast and sure against all, that our own natural reason or the wicked enemy can object or cast in our way.

CHAPTER XXX.

OF THE SACRAMENTS.

To the confirmation of faith and hope serve the holy sacraments of Baptism and of the Supper of the Lord. Baptism is an undoubted true token and evidence of the grace of God, fastened even upon the body; with the which God promiseth and bindeth himself, that he will be thy God and Father for his Son's sake, and will also preserve thee with his own Spirit in thy greatest perils for evermore.

The place of the supper, and persons.

The sacrament of the body and blood of Christ must be exercised and practised only in the coming together of the whole congregation and church, according to the example of the apostles. Therefore let the sick satisfy himself with the general breaking of bread, whereof he was partaker with the whole congregation[1]. But let him diligently consider the

[1 The same opinion is maintained by *Bishop Hooper* in his *Answer to the Bishop of Winchester's Book. Early Writings of Bishop*

fruit thereof, after this manner: God hath promised me his *The fruit of the supper.* grace in Christ, and given me an assured token from heaven in this sacrament, that Christ's life hath in his death overcome my death, and that his obedience in his passion hath destroyed my sins. This godly promise, token, and evidence of my salvation shall not deceive me. I will not suffer this to be taken from me, to die for it. I will rather deny all the world and myself also, than to doubt in God's token and promise. Here the devil tempteth a man to say: " Yea, but through my unworthiness I may spill the gifts of God that are offered me by the word and token, and so be spoiled of the same for ever." Answer: God giveth thee nothing for thine own *Our worthiness to communicate.* worthiness' sake; yea, he buildeth thee unworthy upon the worthiness of his own Son: if thou believe on the Son of God, thou art and continuest worthy before the face of God.

Item: Forasmuch as thou hast gone heretofore unto the Supper of the Lord, thou art through the same sacrament incorporated and conjoined with all them that are sanctified in God, and art already come into the fellowship of the saints, so that they with thee in Christ die and overcome.

CHAPTER XXXI.

OF PRAYER.

No man should presume to exercise faith, and hope, or other spiritual gifts, out of his own power; but humbly to pray unto God for all such things as are needful. And seeing we have need of one mediator and advocate, God hath given *Our sufficiency is from God.* us his Son Jesus Christ. Neither is any of our prayers acceptable unto God, but such as we offer through Jesus Christ. *Heb. xiii.* Therefore must we withdraw ourselves from all creatures, praying and desiring all things at God's hand only through the name of Jesu.

How ought a man to call upon God through Christ? *What is to call upon God in Christ.* With belief that we doubt not but our prayer is heard already.

Hooper, pp. 170—173. Parker Soc. Ed. The objection to the private celebration of the Lord's Supper prevailed at a very early period, as we learn from the second Apology of Justin Martyr, c. 98.]

To such a faith and confidence are we occasioned, in that God hath commanded us to pray, and promised that he will graciously hear us: " Knock, and it shall be opened unto you, &c."

For what thing ought we to make our prayer unto God? For the understanding of his word, for remission of sins, for increase of faith, for love even towards our enemies, for help, patience, comfort, and all spiritual gifts. To pray for health and long life, is not unright, so far as we commit and refer it unto the holy will of God. For we cannot make it better than the faithful Father, that knoweth best of all. And to pray for a long life is ofttimes nothing else than to desire to be kept long in misery. Good Hezekiah yet prayed with tears, that he might live for a season.

Christ, the most perfect example of all, did pray: " Father, if it be possible, take this bitter draught from me; nevertheless, not my will, but thine be done." Like as he now prayed, as the second and third time most earnestly; so ought we also without ceasing to call upon God. Some appoint God beforehand, what death he must suffer them to die. But they do best of all, that prescribe unto the Lord their God neither fashion of death, nor time, neither other circumstance; but refer all unto him, who knoweth what is profitable and good, better than we ourselves.

Moreover, we must pray for wife and child, for friend and enemy, and for the whole congregation of the Christians, that God may graciously take them all into his own protection. Unto prayer belongeth it also, cheerfully to give God thanks for all bodily and ghostly benefits.

The moderation of prayer for temporal things.

Isai. xxxviii.

CHAPTER XXXII.

THE FORM OF PRAYER.

Prayer to God the Father.

O ALMIGHTY everlasting God, merciful Father of heaven, thou hast created me after thine own image, and endowed me with exceeding plentiful gifts. Yet notwithstanding all thy benefits, I have many and sundry ways contemned and transgressed thy commandments. All my days are passed forth with grievous sins. I fear and flee from thee, as from a righteous judge. All this, whatsoever it be, I freely acknowledge and confess, and am sorry for it from the ground of my heart. But, O heavenly Father, I cry and call for thy large and great mercy: O enter not with me into judgment; remember not the sins of my youth. O think upon me according to thy mercy, for thy name's sake, and for thy goodness, which hath been from everlasting. Vouchsafe to grant me thy mercy, which thou according to the contents of the gospel hast promised and opened through thy beloved Son, in such sort, that whoso believeth on him shall have everlasting life. Now is my belief in Jesu Christ, even in the only Redeemer of the whole world. I utterly refuse all other comfort, help, and assistance; and my hope is only through Christ to have pardon of my sins and eternal life. Thy words are true; be it unto me according to thy words: O let me enjoy the passion and death of thine only-begotten Son. Take for my sins the satisfaction and payment of our Lord Jesus Christ, according to the tenor of my belief. Of this my faith thou shalt thyself, O Lord, be witness, and all thine elect. My last will also shall it be, upon thy mercy to die in this faith. Though I now, by occasion of pain, lack of reason, or through temptation should happen or would fall away; suffer me not yet, O Lord, to stick fast in unbelief and blasphemy; but help mine unbelief, strengthen and increase my faith, that sin, death, the devil, and hell do me no harm. Thou art stronger and mightier than they: that is only my trust and confidence.

O Lord, the flesh is feeble and impatient: lay not thou my weakness to my charge, but burn, smite, prick, and plague, as thou wilt thyself; only, I beseech thee, grant me patience and lowliness of mind. Be thou the strength of my soul in this far journey, which I have now to go in an unknown land. Now shew thyself unto my poor soul, so as it may feel that thou art my refuge, my help, protection, defence, comfort, castle, my sure stony rock, my safeguard, my treasure, prosperity, health, and welfare. I yield myself wholly unto thee with soul and body; let me never be confounded. Help also, O heavenly Father, that according unto thy commandment I may love mine enemies, and pray for them that have hurt me; and bring to pass, through thy holy

[margin notes: Confession. Desire of grace. Patience and lowliness is the sign of a Christian. Prayer for the enemy. Matt. v. Rom. xii.]

71

Spirit, that all they whom I have done harm unto, may also forgive me, to the commodity and health of their own souls. For it rueth me, and sorry I am, that at any time I have broken christian love and charity, and beguiled, deceived, or offended any man with evil example, or with too few benefits. I beseech thee, O Lord, through Jesus Christ, forgive thou all them that ever have hurt me in thought, word, or deed.

Prayer for every man.   To thy faithfulness and protection, O dearest Father, I commit all that concerneth me, especially wife, children, friends, and all such as thou hast put under my governance. Comfort and help thou all those that lie in bonds, and are persecuted for thy word's sake.

Have mercy upon all such as are in prison, poverty, sickness, and heaviness. O bring thou the whole world to the knowledge of thy holy word, that they may live according to thy godly will, and throughout all troubles to endure and continue still in the christian faith.

Prayer to God the Son.   O Lord Jesu Christ, I beseech thee, through thine own merits, have mercy upon me. Seeing I myself cannot make satisfaction or sufficient amends towards the Father for my sins, I lay them upon thee, in hope that thou hast already taken them away. For thou hast paid that we ought, and our wounds hast thou healed. O increase thou in me and other men faith, patience, and consolation, what adversity or trouble soever we be in. Thou, Lord Jesu, in thy passion didst pray: "Father, if it be possible, let this cup pass from me: nevertheless, not my will, but thine be done:" and that is my prayer also. Upon the cross thou didst pray: "Father, forgive them." Even so, Lord, forgive I all those that ever have done any thing against me. Thou didst cry: "My God, my God, why hast thou forsaken me?" O Lord, forsake not thou me then in my deadly trouble. Upon the cross thou saidst: "Into thy hands I commend my spirit." Even so now, Lord, commend I my poor soul into thy hands.

Prayer to God the Holy Ghost.   O thou Holy Spirit, great is the anguish and distress of my heart; have mercy upon me for Jesus Christ's sake. I am afflicted, and so are many more: O vouchsafe thou to illuminate, comfort, and strengthen me and them unto all goodness; convey thou and bring us out of all trouble, and fail us not, neither forsake us for evermore. Amen.

CHAPTER XXXIII.

A FORM OF PRAYER AND THANKSGIVING.

O ALMIGHTY, eternal, merciful God and Father, I laud and praise thee, that thou hast created me a reasonable man, and as a Father hast preserved me to this hour; keeping me from great dangers ever since I was born, and doing me more good than ever I was or am worthy. Especially I give thee thanks for thy endless grace, which thou shewest unto me and all faithful, through thy most dear beloved Son; in that he for my sins would be tempted so many ways, and suffer so vile a death, to the intent that I from henceforth might be assured of faithful assistance. *Thanksgiving to God the Father.*

Magnified and blessed be thy name, that thou sufferest me not to die without knowledge of the Holy Ghost. I thank thee also, dearest Father, that thou, visiting me with this sickness and danger, dost not forget me. For in the mean season also thou comfortest and helpest, and full graciously shalt thou bring the matter to an end.

Honour, praise and thanks be unto thee, my most dear Lord Jesu Christ, for thy holy incarnation, for thy martyrdom and bitter passion; whereby I am perfectly assured, that thou art my Redeemer and Saviour. Upon that only set I my building; thitherward standeth my hope; there will I be found cheerfully and gladly; with thy help will I depart hence; trusting that as I am partaker of thy troubles, so shall I also have my part in thy everlasting glory; namely, that at the last day thou shalt raise up this my poor mortal body, taking my soul unto thee immediately at my departing hence. O thou Holy Spirit, I render unto thee praise and thanks for the true understanding, belief, comfort, patience, and all gifts, which thou graciously dost minister and give by the grace of our Lord Jesus Christ. *Thanksgiving to the Son. Rom. vi. Rom. viii. 2 Tim. ii. Thanksgiving to the Holy Ghost.*

CHAPTER XXXIV.

THAT THE PRAYER IS HEARD.

HEREUNTO serve all psalms of prayer and thanksgiving. Howbeit, whatsoever concerneth prayer, it is all comprehended with few words in the holy *Pater-noster*, if it be diligently and earnestly considered. Notwithstanding no christian prayer can be done in vain, that it should not be faithfully heard. Psal. xci. God saith : " He hath a desire unto me, and I will deliver him : when he calleth upon me, I shall hear him ; yea, I am with him in his trouble, whereout I will deliver him, and bring him to honour. He knoweth my name, therefore will I defend him ; with long life will I satisfy him, and shew him my salvation." Yea, the whole Psalter is full of such comfortable promises. Example : if thou pray with the murderer Luke xxiii. upon the cross, that Christ will "remember thee in his kingdom," thou shalt also in thy heart hear the gracious comfort, "This day shalt thou be with me in paradise." Nevertheless, whosoever is in trouble, heaviness, or adversity, ought earnestly to desire the intercessions and prayers of faithful believers.

CHAPTER XXXV.

THAT THE WORD OF GOD OUGHT TO BE PRACTISED AND USED.

FURTHERMORE he ought always to have God's word before his eyes, and fervently to exercise himself therein. For whereas he faithfully calleth unto God, he doeth it upon his word ; and in the word of God he is taught how to behave himself towards all, whatsoever cometh in his way. If a man now cannot give himself true information out of the holy scripture, whether it be concerning sins committed, or other temptations ; then ought he to ask counsel of his learned soul-shepherd, or of some other men of godly understanding. John x. standing. The Lord sayeth not for nought : "My sheep hear my voice, and I know them, and they follow me, and I give them eternal life, and they shall never perish."

CHAPTER XXXVI.

AMENDMENT OF LIFE NECESSARY.

THE true faith bringeth with it naturally a stedfast purpose to live from henceforth according unto all the commandments of God.

Christ also exhorteth every man rightly to exercise and well to use the gifts of God. Hereof bringeth he in a parable: "A certain man, taking a journey into a strange country, [Matt. xxv.] called his servants, and delivered unto them his goods. And unto one he gave five talents, to another two, and to the third one, &c." Upon the same doth the Lord appoint the faithful servant his reward, and punisheth the sluggish and evil servant. The righteousness of faith comprehendeth the fear of God, love of thy neighbour, patience, and all virtue. Of this fear it is written: "The fear of God is a fountain of [Prov. xiv.] life, to avoid the snares of death." Neighbourly love doth first and principally require, that we friendly and unfeignedly, for God's sake, forgive all them that ever have offended us; and again to undertake, as much as lieth in us, to reconcile all our enemies. Then doth charity require to give alms, to comfort the heavy-hearted, and to practise all works of mercy: and look, who hath done thee good in thy sickness, it is requisite that thou give them thanks. Among benefits this is not the least, when one moveth and exhorteth another to keep himself from all filthiness. As for bodily things, the sick should dispatch them with few words; but such as concern our honesty, the fear of God, safeguard in him, and the homage which is due unto him, that ought to be done with more deliberation. For look, what one speaketh at the point of death, the same goeth deeper to the heart of such as hear it; partly, because it cannot be thought, that a man on his death bed, being in greatest trouble, will use hypocrisy, or dissemble; partly, for that when the soul beginneth to be discharged of the body, it ofttimes sheweth some token of the freedom and joy, with the which it shall, even now forthwith, be perfectly endowed. Example: the dear worthy patriarchs in the old Testament, before their departing out of this life, sent and called for their children and other folks, instructing and exhorting them to submit themselves unto the

[1 Macc. ii.] law of God, and diligently to walk therein. How faithfully did Mattathias at his death speak to his noble sons, comforting them out of God's word against all their enemies.

CHAPTER XXXVII.

EXHORTATION UNTO PATIENCE.

FINALLY, we cannot do better than with God's help, being patient in all adversity, and stedfast in all temptations, most gently and meekly to give over our wills into the will of God. I speak not of such a patience and valiantness, as utterly to feel no more terror of death; for that is a very blockish unsensibleness of wild, mad, barbarous people: but all such feebleness as is felt, must a christian man overcome, and with faithful confidence upon the grace of God cheerfully step forth before the eyes of death.

In the passion and death of Christ we have a perfect example, not only of patience, but also of every other thing, that hitherto is written concerning preparation unto death.

For he is given unto us of God not only to be our re-
1 Cor. i.
Coloss. ii.
demption; but also to be unto us wisdom, whereby we must learn all that is necessary for our health.

The seven words that the Lord spake upon the cross, are specially to be pondered, weighed, and considered.

The first: "Father, forgive them, for they wot not what they do."

The second: "Woman, lo! there is thy son."

The third: "This day shalt thou be with me in paradise."

The fourth: "My God, my God, why hast thou forsaken me?"

The fifth: "I am athirst."

The sixth: "It is finished."

The seventh: "Father, into thy hands I commend my spirit."

Examples of saints.
Through the knowledge of Jesus Christ did all holy fathers and servants of God in the old and new Testament give over themselves willingly unto death, the way of all
Luke ii.
flesh. Holy Simeon saith: "Lord, now lettest thou thy servant depart in peace, according to thy word: for mine

76

eyes have seen thy salvation, which thou hast prepared before the face of all people, &c."

Seeing then that every faithful Christian doth no less see A lesson to learn to die. Christ with the eyes of his heart; he ought with praise and thanks to say: " Forasmuch as I am assured and do constantly believe, that I am redeemed and delivered by Jesus Christ, and not destroyed, but only changed through the death of the body; I am right willing and well content to depart hence and to die, whensoever now it shall please the Lord my God."

The murderer upon the cross did willingly suffer the death that he had deserved; and so he obtained the everlasting triumph of a martyr.

Holy Steven was content to suffer the fierce cruelty of the enemies; for in his last trouble he knelt down and cried with a loud voice: " Lord Jesu, receive my spirit; Lord, lay Acts vii. not this sin to their charge."

Paul, the chosen vessel of God, speaketh thus very comfortable : " My desire is to be loosed, to depart hence out of Phil. i. misery, and to be with Christ, which thing is best of all : for Christ is to me life, and death is to me advantage."

These and such noble examples of other holy martyrs should by reason provoke us feeble sluggish Christians to be the more hardy and stout, and to think thus : Well, go to, thou hast as yet suffered no great thing for the Lord Christ's sake ; therefore now, even as a lamb, give over thyself cheerfully unto death for his name's sake.

Thou hast daily made thy prayer, as Christ hath taught Prayer requireth thee, that God will take thee out of this wicked world into patience. his kingdom, and that his will be done. Now if he will Matt. vi. graciously convey thee into his kingdom, thou oughtest from the bottom of thy heart to rejoice, and as his own child, willingly to obey them.

Forasmuch as the famous heathen man, Socrates, being before the seat of judgment, where the matter touched his body and life, desired no advocate, neither submitted himself to the judges, but valiantly disputed before them, and proved that there is no evil in death ; it should sound very evil, if we (which out of the infallible word of God are instructed concerning a better life) should forsake this life of misery with less patience, and with more unquietness of mind, than died the heathen man.

CHAPTER XXXVIII.

THE ORIGINAL AND FRUIT OF PATIENCE.

To the intent that the feebleness of our nature, which quaketh at death as at a thing terrible, may shew christian patience, we must cleave unto Jesus Christ with true faith, which shall warm our hearts to have a love and desire after the heavenly glory and everlasting salvation; yea, rather to lose an hundred bodies, if it were possible, than to be destitute of the holy gospel, whereby we are assured of deliverance from sin, devil, and hell, by means of the blood-shedding of Jesus Christ.

Gen. xv.
Rom. iv.
Gal. iii.
Gen. xii. xx.
and xxvi.

Impatient folks grudge against God, pouring out all unthankfulness, for that they were not created immortal; and so imagine they in themselves a terrible cruel God; yea, all manner of vices grow out of impatiency. Abraham, who otherwise is set forth for an example of faith and righteousness, fearing death too sore, sinned grievously, denying Sara to be his wife.

Note this
well. What
christian
heart can
read this
without
tears?

In these latter days (the more pity, God be merciful unto us!) it is become a common thing, for fear of death, to carry the true belief only in heart secret, outwardly to deny the holy gospel, and with mouth, behaviour, and gesture to serve antichrist.

CHAPTER XXXIX.

THAT A MAN, WHILE HE IS YET IN HEALTH, OUGHT TO PREPARE HIMSELF BEFOREHAND.

THIS preparation ought no man to linger or defer till another time, though he be never so whole and sound; but every one forthwith and daily to begin to make himself for death, to the intent that at all hours he may be found ready. Like as a stout and valiant soldier, when he must be up and fight with the enemies, oversleepeth not himself, but keepeth his standing, and hath his weapons and harness already upon him; so much more ought we Christians at all times to wait

upon our heavenly Captain, when he bloweth the trump, that
we may be ready to pass forth with him. "Let your loins Luke xii.
be girded about and your lights burning, and ye yourselves
like unto men that wait for their master, when he will return
from the wedding; that as soon as he cometh and knocketh, they may open unto him immediately. Happy are
those servants, whom the Lord, when he cometh, shall find
waking."

With this similitude doth Christ exhort every man, that
at all times we prepare ourselves against his coming, when he
knocketh through sickness and other dangers; when he calleth
us out of this life; and when he shall come again out of his
heavenly palace to judge the living and the dead. The right
preparation is true faith, fervent love and charity, the clear
shine of all virtues, and specially a gentle willing mind to
open unto the Lord, to let him in, and with him to pass into
his royal and matrimonial palace of the everlasting joyful
kingdom.

The preacher saith: "Remember thy Maker in thy youth, Eccl. xii.
or ever the days of adversity come, and before the years
draw nigh, when thou shalt say, I am weary of my life."
Again we read: "Examine and correct thyself, before the Wisd. xviii.
judgment come: so shalt thou find grace in the sight of God.
Humble thyself before thou be sick, and declare in season
that thou wilt cease from sin. Be not hindered to pray in
due time, and defer not thy amendment until death." No man
knoweth the time, place, or manner, how he shall end this
life. Many one hopeth yet long to live, and thinketh, "I am
yet young, I will follow the world. When I am old, or have
a wife and keep house, then will I begin to frame myself."
But, O thou fool! who hath promised thee that thou shalt be
an old man, yea, that thou shalt live to-morrow? As nothing
is more certain than death, so is nothing more uncertain than
the hour of death, which the Lord hath not opened to his
best friends. Therefore every day think thou none other A friendly
in thy mind, but that thy glass is run out: let every day be warning.
unto thee the last day, seeing thou wotest not whether thou
shalt live till to-morrow. Learn to beware by the example of
other men, upon whom stretch-leg came suddenly, and slew
them, even when they thought nothing less than to die.

Yea, of death ought we to think, as of that which is

present : for we have death by the foot, and carry him about with us in our whole body.

Like as one in a ship, whether he sit, stand, awake or asleep, is ever still borne and carried forward, although he mark it not greatly, neither feel it; so our life in a continual motion doth every twinkling of an eye steal forth, and privily creep to the end, though we mark not how the time passeth.

Psal. xc. David saith: "Our time goeth forth swiftly, as though we did fly." As if he would say, there can nothing run or fly Wisd. xiv. away more swiftly. And Sirac saith: "Remember that death tarrieth not."

Cor. xv. Paul saith: "I die daily." For even "in the midst of life are we in death:" yea, death daily, as soon as we are born, taketh away somewhat of our life. After this meaning writeth Augustine: "The time of this life is nothing else but a rounding unto death[1]."

Moreover, death is daily set before our eyes: we hear the sighing and lamentable voices of them that die; we see the corses carried to the burial; we go by the graves of the dead; we be still talking of those that are dead and buried.

If the example of others touch us but a little, then let us consider ourselves. Where is there one of us, that hath not sometime been in danger of life, either through tempest, sickness, pestilence, murder, war, or other misfortune? Therefore seeing death waiteth for us on every side; we do wisely, when we also on every side wait for him, that he take us not unprepared, or catch us suddenly. Though a man perfectly knew, (as no man doth indeed,) that it should be long before he died; yet were it exceeding dangerous to defer the preparation till then. And more profitably could not one handle the matter, than by time and in due season to direct himself unto that place, where he desireth everlastingly to remain. For uncertain he is, when the last hour cometh, whether he shall convert himself to God, and whether he shall have his right mind, or not.

Though he be not robbed of his right mind, yet in deadly sickness he hath so much to do with the trouble, that it is hard then for him to learn that he hath not comprehended and learned before. The unspeakable pain of the body, the

[1 Præsens vita fragilis est, et in mortem proclivis.—Augustin. *De verbis Domini.* Sermo xxv. Opera, Vol. x. 24. E. Ed. 1541.]

horrible sight of thine own sins, the terrible fear of God's judgment, and the cruel temptation of the devil, come altogether upon one heap in the perturbance and cumbrance of death, and hinder exceeding much in every thing that one ought to think, speak, or do. If thou now hast lightly regarded all warning, and so diest in thy sins, thou shalt not be able after death to amend any more. All repentance and sorrowing from that time forth shall be in vain. When the ungodly dieth, his hope is gone. Forasmuch then as it is so, that in death we must abide the sorest and most dangerous conflict and battle; every reasonable man may well perceive, that we ought by time and season, yea, all our life-time, to prepare beforehand against the said battle.

CHAPTER XL.

THAT THE FORESAID THINGS OUGHT BY TIME AND IN DUE SEASON TO BE TAKEN IN HAND.

THY last will and testament being made, while thy body is whole and sound, causeth not thee to die the sooner, as our feeble understanding imagineth; but is an occasion that thou diest the more quietly, and that thou then goest not first about such thorns, when thou liest upon thy death-bed. Well done is it, when one that dieth doth restore evil-gotten goods: but unto God it is a hundred times more acceptable, if thou restore it thyself, while thou art whole and sound in body. It is well done to bestow one portion of goods for the relief of the poor: but yet it is a much more acceptable offering unto God, when one himself in his lifetime giveth unto the poor. For that which thou upon thy death-bed appointest for them, is not always distributed; and though it be, yet is it no more thine. Some do even as the wife, that would give none of her pottage to any body, till her pot was overthrown; then called she the poor unto it.

It is well done in the end to forgive all men, and to pray unto God that he also will forgive all thine enemies:

The fruit of making thy testament in time of health.

but much more commendable is it to forgive them before, while thou hast thy health, and not do it for fear of death, but for the very love of Christ. As for other weighty matters wherewith thou art wrapped, concerning wife, children, neighbours, debts, friends, or enemies, those likewise oughtest not thou to defer till the last day, wherein thou hast enough to do with the world, which thou art loath to forsake; with death, whom naturally thou hatest; with the devil, who practiseth all his crafty falsehood and subtlety; with the fear of hell, the terror whereof is horrible. By means of such things an unprepared man doth oft forget the grace of God and the soul's health. For if thou, having alway a loving friend in estimation, doest contrariwise little regard a poor neighbour; it were no wonder, if thou shouldst forget the same neighbour in the mean season, when thy dear friend is departed. Even so, when one now hath alway cast what may do the body good, howsoever it goeth with the soul, no marvel that the soul's health is neglected, when the body faileth.

After this meaning doth holy Augustine earnestly threaten, saying: "With this penalty is a sinner punished, that when he dieth he forgetteth himself, who in his life-time thought not upon God." Therefore while a man is in his flowers of health, he ought in such sort to learn the comfortable sayings of the gospel, that in his trouble they may of themselves fall into his mind; or if other men advertise him of them, he may be the better acquainted with them, and have them on his finger's end, as them that he hath known, exercised, and used before.

Moreover faith, whereby we overcome death and hell, hath her beginning, increase, and strength, and is direct not only above, but also against all the natural reason of man, that the infinite eternal God should freely, of a very gracious favour through his dear Son, take our part that are most grievous sinners. Therefore by times and in due season, through the preaching of the word, through the prayer and sacrament, should faith in us be planted, increased, practised, and made perfect.

In the mean time, as long as we live, ought we to pray and beseech God of a gracious hour and blessed end; and when the end draweth nigh, to put God in remembrance of the same prayer, as well as of his commandment and promise, in that he hath not only charged us to pray, but promised also that he will graciously hear us.

Daily ought we to have remorse of conscience, where as we have failed, to repent and be sorry, to crave of God forgiveness, and to take upon us immediately to amend all such things as are amiss. For in the sight of God it is a thousand times more acceptable to cease from evil by time in due season, before trouble come, than that present danger and fear should force us to amendment. *Oh most gracious God, give us grace to do this, and with unfeigned hearts to put it in practice.*

He that is fallen into a deep foggy well, and sticketh fast in it, will he not straightway call unto every man to help him out one way or another? Will he not make a sore moan, howsoever men haste to deliver him? Out of doubt he that goeth above with sin and vice, hangeth by a bare weak thread, so to say, above the pit of hell; yea, he is now in hell already, forasmuch as he turneth not from sin to the grace of God.

Then must it needs be an horrible, devilish, and obstinate blindness, when one sticketh fast in such a state of life, as is altogether cursed, and yet will appoint a day a great while hence for to come, and therein think to begin to give the devil his leave; when he knoweth not himself, whether he shall live till that day, and whether he shall then have a mind to convert.

For to have a will unto true repentance, is a free gift of God, which ought of him daily to be desired, that the common proverb be not verified in us: "Vicious life, unhappy death." He that will lie well and soft, must make his bed hereafter. Yet for all this it is not my mind to shut up the grace of God into a narrow strait, or to bid any man despair. When an evil-disposed man, that feareth not God, lieth upon his death-bed, being afraid of hell and damnation, he may happen to desire of God longer life, for this intent that he may afterward amend, become a better man, and more directed to die. But let not such vain thoughts trouble thee. For though thou shouldst live yet an hundred years longer, thou mightest through thine own perfectness deserve nothing toward God. But be thou of this assured without all doubt,

that there can no true repentance come too late. Turn thee
yet, even this present day, unto God; be heartily and unfeignedly sorry for thy sins; be of a good mind and whole
purpose, that if God help thee up again, thou wilt amend
all things. Nevertheless comfort thyself by that only mean
which God hath prescribed; namely, the Lord Jesus. So
shalt thou be sure, with the murderer upon the cross, to have
gracious favour for ever.

THE

SECOND BOOK OF DEATH.

CHAPTER I.

HOW THE SICK OUGHT TO BE SPOKEN UNTO, IF NEED SHALL REQUIRE.

HITHERTO have we declared, how one ought to use himself in the dangers of body and life.

Now followeth, how we should behave ourselves towards them that be in like case. Hereof did David sing these words in the 41st Psalm: " Blessed is he that considereth or thinketh upon the poor; for in the time of trouble the Lord shall deliver him. The Lord shall preserve him and save his life; he shall make him prosper upon earth, and shall not deliver him into the will of his enemies. When he himself lieth sick upon his bed, the Lord shall refresh him; yea, thou, Lord, makest his bed in all his sickness." Item, he that is judge of us all shall at the latter day pronounce this sentence: " Come, ye blessed of my Father, possess the kingdom that hath been prepared for you from the beginning of the world. For I was sick, and ye visited me." O what a wicked unbelief is this, that we are more afraid at a little adversity and uncertain danger, than encouraged by such a godly, sure, and faithful promise !

Therefore among the greatest works of mercy this is reckoned, to visit the sick, to have compassion on them, to give them good counsel, and to comfort them. Which thing must be done with reason and discretion, to the intent that neither too little nor too much be meddled withal. Too little were it, to cause the sick still to believe, that he shall shortly come up again and recover. For such fond hope have men already of their own nature, and thereby sometime .they oversee themselves.

85

Again, it were too much to deal roughly with one that is weak of faith, and suddenly to fear him with death: that were even as much as to break the bruised reed, and utterly to quench the smoking flax, contrary to the example of Christ our Lord.

A whole instruction ought to be given unto such sick persons as have need thereof, to make them strong and willing unto the cross and death. And so should they also be put in mind, what death is, whence it came, and wherefore, what it doeth through the grace of God for Christ's sake, by whose Spirit and power the most horrible death of all is overcome. Hereof is spoken sufficiently in the chapters going before.

Out of the which foundation, it may thus be spoken unto the sick: "Thou hast the Almighty God thy dear Father, and Jesus Christ thine intercessor and Saviour, who hath taken all thy cause in hand; let him alone withal; he will not suffer thee to perish, but give thee his holy Spirit, which shall conduct thee into eternal joy and salvation. Only direct thou thyself even now at this present, and prepare thee to depart, giving all temporal things their leave, having a right understanding of the holy gospel, and exercising the true belief thereof by fervent prayer, charitable love, and patience.

"Turn thee, for God's sake, from all creatures to the Creator and Maker; turn thee from wife and child, turn thee from temporal goods and honour, considering that none of them can help thee, neither from sin, nor from death. All that thou leavest behind thee, the Lord according to his almighty providence shall well and fatherly take care for them. He that hath created thy wife and children, shall also provide them a living, as he hath sent unto thee all things necessary, even unto this hour."

Afterward ought not the mind of the sick to be disturbed or pointed hither and thither, up and down, as (the more pity!) they use to do in the papistry; but only unto God the Father through Jesus Christ, according to the contents of The spiritual the whole gospel, after this meaning: "Dost thou believe comforter. and confess from the ground of thy heart, that there is but one only God, who hath given thee body and soul, meat and drink, lodging and clothing, with all other necessaries, and graciously helped thee out of many grievous mischances and miseries?" Then let the sick say: "Yea, that I acknowledge and confess." _{The sick.}

"Dost thou also confess that thou oughtest, above all things, to have feared and worshipped this thy gracious Maker and Father, and to have loved him with all thy heart, with all thy soul, with all thy strength, and, for his sake, thy neighbour as thyself? Hath not God deserved that at thy hand?" Then let him say: "O Lord God, I should indeed have done so." _{The comforter. / The sick.}

"Acknowledge thou likewise, that thou oft and many a time hast wittingly and willingly, of very ungraciousness, done against God and thy neighbour; by means whereof thou hast justly deserved the everlasting wrath, plague, and indignation of God in body and soul." Then let him say: "O sir, it is all too true; I yield myself guilty, and confess it before God." "Well, greater and more horrible sins than these couldst not thou do, if thou wouldst still not regard the wrath and rigorous judgment of God, as thou hast done heretofore. How art thou minded? Dost thou desire and pray from the ground of thy heart, that God will preserve thee from such slender regarding of thine own sins, and of his just wrath and judgment? Desirest thou also with thy whole heart, that God will not deal with thee after his divine judgment and justice, but according to his fatherly mercy, and that he will remit and forgive thy sins and trespasses?" Then let him say: "Yea, that is my desire from the bottom of my heart." _{The comforter. / The sick. / The comforter. / The sick.}

"God from heaven did send unto thee his dear and only-begotten Son, who took upon him the nature of man, and in his death upon the cross he bare not only our trespass, but the pain also and punishment due for the same, making full payment and satisfaction for us. John the Baptist with his finger pointeth unto Christ, and sayeth: 'Lo, this is God's Lamb, that taketh away the sin of the world.' And John the evangelist saith: 'The blood of Jesus Christ cleanseth us from all sin.' Dost thou now confess, that Jesus Christ, the Son of God, died and rose again for thee also? And wilt thou, as one parcel of the world, one broken reed, one piece of smoking flax, and one lost sheep, cast all thy sins upon him; embracing this comfort _{The comforter. / 1 John i.}

of the gospel in thy heart, and comprehending it with a strong stedfast belief?" Then let him say: "O Lord Jesu, my heart's desire is of thee to be healed, comforted, and refreshed. And thanks be unto God for evermore, that I may have him my mediator and redeemer! I will wholly commit and yield myself unto him."

"Then, upon this, the Lord Jesus Christ by his godly word and gospel sendeth thee this message: 'Thy sins are forgiven thee, and in his sight are all taken away: not only the sin, but the pain also due for the same; namely, everlasting death, hell, and damnation: so that thou shalt be received again as a dear acceptable child, and heir of eternal life.' Believest thou this comfortable promise of Jesu Christ?"

Then let him say: "Yea, but, O merciful God, strengthen thou my weak belief."

The sum of all this is contained in the articles of the christian belief, which, with the aforesaid interpretation, may be rehearsed unto the sick.

"And to the intent that thy heart may be set at rest, and thou assured in thy faith, therefore hath Christ instituted his holy Supper and sacrament of his body and blood; wherein he doth signify, witness, and put to his seal, that even thou also art one of those many, for whom he gave his body and shed his blood. Now when sin, death, hell, devil, and God's wrath tempteth and turmoileth thy conscience, thou must with the same sacrament, as with the word of God, comfort thy conscience, that Christ Jesus with his body and life is thy surety; and that his soul and blood, and all that he is, standeth for thee and on thy side, against all bodily and ghostly enemies."

Moreover, thou must bid the sick call upon God for faith, patience, and other spiritual gifts.

Some time recite before him the Lord's Prayer, with a short exposition, that he may direct his prayer the better.

Exhort also all such as stand about the sick to pray for him, considering that our Lord hath made a rich and faithful promise: "Where two or three are assembled in his name, he himself will be in the midst among them, and grant them their desire."

And forasmuch as all instructions must be taken of the word of God, therefore before the sick these parcels following may be read.

The vi. Psalm, which beginneth: "Lord, rebuke me not in thine anger," &c.

The xxii. "My God, my God," &c.

The xxv. "Unto thee, O Lord," &c.

The xxvii. "The Lord is my light," &c.

The xlii. "Like as the hart longeth," &c.

The li. "Have mercy upon me," &c.

The xci. "Whoso dwelleth," &c.

The cxvi. "I am well pleased," &c.

The cxxxix. "O Lord, thou searchest me," &c.

The cxliii. "Hear my prayer, O Lord," &c.

The Prayer of King Hezekiah: Isaiah xxxviii.

The Psalm of Simeon: "Nunc dimittis."   Luke ii.

The xi. chapter of John; of Lazarus.

The xiv. and xvii. of St John's gospel.

The Passion of Christ, and specially concerning the one of the two murderers.

The viii. chapter to the Romans.

The 1 Corinthians xv.   All which places serve to make the prayer fervent, and to strengthen true belief.

Furthermore, the sick ought to be told of the fruits of faith, because of provoking thankfulness for the unspeakable grace of God; with exhortation to forgive his enemies, to do every man good according to his power, and in every point to amend his own life and conversation; but especially with a patient, gentle, quiet, and good willing mind to wait for deliverance.

Namely thou mayest say thus: "Take up thy cross upon thy neck patiently, and follow Christ thy Lord. Remember, and behold Christ hanging in great martyrdom upon the cross. He suffered patiently until his Father's will was fulfilled in him. Even so thou also hold still unto the Lord thy God, that he may perform his will in thee: if it be his good pleasure now to take the stinking transitory flesh from thee, to purify it, and to make an eternal glorified body of it, thou hast great cause to rejoice."

When the sick is drawing away, and speechless, having yet understanding, thou mayest speak unto him these words: *At the point of death.* "Fight valiantly, as a worthy Christian, and despair not; be not afraid of the rigorous judgment of God; hold thee fast to the comfortable promise of Christ, thereas he saith: 'I am the Resurrection and the Life. He that believeth on me shall live, though he were dead; and whoso liveth and believeth on me, shall never die.' In him is thy belief; therefore shalt thou live with him for ever. Christ thy Saviour shall never forsake thee. There can no man pluck thee out of his hand. Heaven and earth shall pass, but God's word endureth for ever. Have thou therefore no doubt, thou shalt after this battle receive the crown of everlasting life."

John x.
Luke xxi.

Ask now the man, whether he understand and believe; desire a token of him, and cry unto him fair and softly: "Good brother, upon thy soul's health depart not, shrink not away from Jesus Christ; commit thy soul unto thy faithful God and loving Father. Speak from thy heart-root with Christ thy brother upon the cross: 'Father, into thy hands, into thy protection and defence, I commit my spirit.'"

When his understanding is past, commit him unto God. Make thy prayer alone, or with others, that God will take this sick man into eternal life, and grant him a joyful resurrection at the last day, only for the Lord Jesus Christ's sake. Amen.

CHAPTER II.

OF THE BURIAL, AND WHAT IS TO BE DONE TOWARDS THOSE THAT ARE DEPARTED HENCE.

THE soul of the dead, as soon as it is departed from hence, cometh into a state there, as prayers (if one would make them for him afterward) have no place, and are either unprofitable, or else vain; yea, offensive also, and hindrance to our christian belief.

The body of him that is departed ought reverently and soberly to be conducted unto the earth, and buried. For that is the last service that we can do for such as are departed, and thereby may we declare our charitable love towards them. In the mean season, when we reverently commit the body, as the wheat corn, unto the earth, we testify our belief of the resurrection for to come. The scripture also commendeth those that faithfully will have to do with burying of the dead,

after the example of Tobias. Of misordering the bodies of
the dead writeth Plato, the heathen philosopher: "Is it not
a bond, greedy and voluptuous thing, to spoil the dead corpse,
and to rage against the body as an enemy, when the enemy
that fought in the body is departed away? What differ
they from dogs, which bite the stone that is cast at them,
and let him go free that cast it? There is no difference.
Of such points ought we to beware, for they bring hurt unto
victory."

Of gorgeous graves and sepulchres, it is written in the
poet Euripides: "Men's minds are mad, when they bestow
vain cost upon dead bodies[1]." For if we consider the matter
right, we must needs greatly marvel, that ever a man should
fall into such a frensy, as to use pride after death.

Touching the place of burial, it is to be noted, that by
such ordinary means as be permitted us we are bound to
avoid sickness and all hurt. Now out of graves there come
naturally evil savours or vapours, which alter and change
the air, and increase the disease of the pestilence, when the
church-yard or place of burial standeth in the midst of cities
or towns. Therefore both the Jews, heathen, and Christians,
were wont to have their burials without the cities. For what
time as Christ raised the widow's son from death, the evangelist saith: "When he came nigh unto the gate of the city, Luke vii.
behold, there was carried out one dead, who was the only
son of his mother, she being a widow, and much people of
the city with her." Moreover the sepulchre of our Lord
Jesus Christ was without the city. But the pope and his
adherents with their money market found here a treasure
bag, otherwise persuading the people; as though to lie here
or there did further or hinder salvation.

Afterward let the dead rest quietly, no evil being spoken Good
of them of malice, but good, though they were our enemies: counsel.
of malice, I say; for otherwise must vice and sin, as well of
the dead as of the living, be declared and rebuked, that others
may beware. The old poet Mimnermus writeth: "We are
all inclined to envy an excellent famous man, but after death

[1 Ἀνθρώπων δὲ μαίνονται φρένες,
δαπάνας ὅταν θανοῦσι πέμπωσιν κενάς.
Euripides, Polyid. Fragm. v.]

91

to praise him[1]." Therefore do they not only against christian charity, but also against man's nature, that disdain to give unto the dead their due praise and commendation.

Especially when one that hath shewed us friendship and kindness is departed, we ought never to forget his benefits, but to declare our thankfulness to his kinsfolks or friends. But if we carry the remembrance of them to the grave, and bury it with the corpse, thinking no more upon their gentleness; then are we like unto wild beasts, that are hot and burning in desire, but as soon as the thing desired is out of sight, the love is quenched. Hereof complaineth the poet Euripides : " Seldom are there found faithful constant friends after death, though aforetime they were joined never so near together." The thankfulness that is shewed to him that is present passeth away and vanisheth, when one is carried out of the house.

[1] Δεινοὶ γὰρ ἀνδρὶ πάντες ἐσμὲν εὐκλεεῖ
ζῶντι φθονῆσαι, κατθανόντα δ' αἰνέσαι.
Mimnermus apud Brunck. Analecta.]

THIRD BOOK OF DEATH.

CHAPTER I.

HOW THEY OUGHT TO BE COMFORTED, WHOSE DEAR FRIENDS ARE DEAD.

NATURALLY we mourn, weep, and lament, when our kinsfolk and friends depart.   When father and mother dieth, the son and the daughter remembereth, how many a footstep the elders went faithfully and worthily to provide them their living: yea, if it had been possible, they would have shewed the child their own soul, and given them the heart in their body.

Again, the parents consider how good obedient children they have had of their sons or daughters; and what honour and joyfulness more they might have had of their children, if they should have lived longer.

The sisters and brothers remember, that they came of one father, being born under one motherly heart, brought up in one house, eating and drinking at one table.   If it were else a man's companion, he thinketh, he was my faithful dear friend, he did no man hurt nor harm, but desired to do every man service, and that so honestly, that a man might have trusted him with his own soul.

If he were a good ruler, we think he was to his own native country true and faithful, and excellently well inclined to the welfare thereof; who hath not then good cause to be sorry for his departing?   This is the cause, that the blood naturally gathereth together, so that we are sorrier for the death of such one than of another private man.

Such heaviness, pity, and compassion doth God allow. For he hath not created us to be stones and blocks, but hath given us five senses, and made us an heart of flesh, that we might have feeling, and love our friends, being sorry when they suffer trouble and die : yea, God hateth unfriendly and unmerciful people, and whose hearts are not moved, when their friends are vexed and taken away from them. There-Gen. xxiii. fore the holy patriarch Abraham lamented and mourned for Sarah his wife, when she was dead.

Gen l. Good Joseph made great lamentation for Jacob his father.

Phil. ii. Paul likewise writeth thus : " My helper and fellow-soldier Epaphroditus was deadly sick : but God had mercy upon him, and not only upon him, but also upon me, that I should not have one heaviness upon another." But as in all things, so in this there ought a measure to be kept, that we continue not in fleshly inordinate heaviness, but still resist the sorrow, and comfort ourselves with this account following: What do we mean thus to mourn and lament? What will we do ? The Lord is great, and doeth no man wrong. And the same is an honest good will, that conformeth itself to the will of God.

For the good heathen man Seneca wrote unto his scholar A notable saying. Lucillus after this manner : " A man ought to be content with every thing that God is pleased withal, only because it pleased God."

Now is every thing ordered by the providence of God, Lib. v. cap. as holy Augustine, *De Civitate Dei*, saith, " Without an 2. orderly division and convenient joining together of the parts hath not God left so much as the bowels of any beast, how vile or small so ever the same be, nor the feathers of a bird, nor the flower of the herb, neither the leaf of the tree : so that there can nothing be found, that is not subject to the providence of God[1]; neither can there any little bird die, without his device, charge, and commandment."

[1 The author, according to his custom, has applied the passage of Augustine, to which reference is made by him, to the purposes of his argument: Deus summus et verus cum Verbo suo et Spiritu sancto, quæ tria unum sunt, Deus unus et omnipotens, creator et factor omnis animæ atque omnis corporis,... qui non solum cœlum et terram, nec solum angelum et hominem, sed nec exigui et contemptibilis animantis viscera, nec avis pennulam, nec herbæ flosculum, nec arboris folium sine suarum partium convenientia et quadam veluti pace dereliquit, nullo modo est credendus regna hominum eorumque dominationes et servitutes a suæ providentiæ legibus alienas esse voluisse. Augustin. *De Civitate Dei.* Lib. v. cap. 11. Oper. Vol. v. p. 44. D. Ed. Par. 1541.]

If God now have so diligent respect to such small things, how then could thy friend, whom thou mournest for, depart away by death without the providence of God? Therefore if we speak against the Lord's works, and cry against his will, what is that else, but even as though we therefore lived upon earth, that we as lords and rulers should prescribe laws for the Almighty? Which thing to think, I will not say to speak, were yet horrible.

When thou givest forth thy child to a nurse, and she hath kept it long enough, thou takest it home again; the nurse having no reasonable cause to complain upon thee, for taking again thine own. Yet much less cause have we to grudge against God our creditor, when he by death taketh his own again. For as for father and mother, brother and sister, wife and child, friend and lover, yea, and all other things that we have, what are they else but lent goods and free gifts of God, which he hath committed unto us, and which we, as long as he lendeth us them, ought to esteem as advantage?

When a lord hath lent us a fair costly table, whether should we gladly with thanks restore it him again when he requireth it, or brawl with him after this manner: O thou terrible lord, how happeneth it that thou hast robbed us of so costly a table? How cometh it that thou hast taken it from us again so suddenly? Upon such a complaint might he not with good right answer: Is that now my reward for lending you so costly a table, which I did of love, undeserved on your part, that ye might have commodity and pleasure thereof for a while? Yea, the more worthy the gift was that I lent you to use, the more thankful should you be unto me. Yea, with rougher words might God justly rebuke us that be so impatient. When the house fell upon Job's ten living children, seven sons and three daughters, and when his seven thousand sheep were burned with fire from heaven, and his enemies carried away his five hundred yoke of oxen and five hundred asses, as the other enemies drove away three hundred camels, and slew also his servants; in all this misery and hurt Job comforteth himself, and thanketh God, who had lent him such things, and taken them away again. "The Lord," saith he, "hath given them, the Lord hath Job i. taken them; even as it hath pleased the Lord, so is it come

95

to pass: blessed be the name of the Lord." Let us therefore also say with Job: " The Lord gave us this father, that child, such a friend; the Lord hath taken him again; blessed be his name."

But when thou shouldst laud and praise God, it hindereth thee exceedingly, if thou fear that God of a wrath and enmity against thee hath taken away from thee thy son or thy wife, &c. Such an opinion cometh not of God, but is even a practice of the devil. And herewith agreeth our feeble nature: whatsoever is sung or said, we think in trouble, that God is angry, and that our will is good and profitable, and not God's will.

Contrary hereunto are we instructed by holy scripture, that though we know not perfectly for what cause God sendeth us this or that punishment, yet ought we to be satisfied in this, that God is gracious and favourable unto us for his beloved Son our Lord Jesus Christ's sake. Nevertheless, to the intent that we may both the better understand, and be the more glad to receive, the good-will of God, I will declare what profit such a death bringeth to him that departeth and to those that remain.

CHAPTER II.

THAT UNTO SUCH AS DIE, IT IS PROFITABLE TO DEPART OUT OF THIS LIFE.

IF they that be dead from hence had not suffered trouble in this world when they were alive, it were no marvel to see us mourn out of measure for their departing. As for all their joy and pastime upon earth, they are scarce to be accounted dreams, in comparison of the true joys and treasures above. Again: who will undertake to number the adversities that all men, of what estate soever they be, must be possessors [Job xiv.] of? We may well say with Job: " Man that is born of a woman, liveth but a short time, and is replenished with many miseries." Against the which there helpeth neither gold nor silver, neither power nor nobility, neither policy nor natural wit. To-day we are whole and sound, to-morrow sick; to-day merry, to-morrow sorry; to-day rich, to-morrow poor;

to-day honoured, to-morrow despised; to-day alive, to-morrow dead.

Moreover, vice commonly hath so the upper hand, that none can live upon earth, but he must displease either God or man, or else them both. Therefore seeing thy loving friend is gotten out of the mire, and gone out of the sweat-bath that thou yet sittest in; art thou sorry now that he is released and unburdened of so much misery? Thou shouldst rather give thanks and praise unto God for it; specially forasmuch as death doth utterly destroy neither body nor soul, neither honesty nor virtue, wherein he that is now departed did here exercise himself in time. For look, what good thing one hath done, it shall not be quenched out through death; but the praise and commendation thereof, among all such as are good, doth rather increase than diminish after death. The soul departing in true faith, passeth straight to the joy of heaven.

The least parcel of the body doth not utterly perish, but the whole body shall at the last day be called to immortality, where our friends shall be a thousand times better, richer, more pleasant, and more blessed, than ever they were upon earth; when we all shall come to them again, see them, know them, and have perpetual company with them and all saints. After this sort did Adam and Eve trust that Abel, who was slain, should be restored again unto them, because of the Seed that was promised.

A similitude: if a great lord had called thee and thy son, and promised you much wealth and good, shouldst thou weep when thy son goeth to him, and thou thyself wilt shortly follow after? No, verily; but thou wouldst order thy matter so that thou mightest be there out of hand. Why unquietest thou thyself then so sore for the death of thy son or friend? The Almighty Lord hath called him and thee to his eternal kingdom, to place thee and him among the princes of heaven. Thy son passeth hence through the gates of death; he shall rise again to honour. Why vexest thou then thyself? Why orderest not thou thyself, joyfully to follow him? for thou hast not lost him, but only sent him before.

If it were possible that thy son knew of thy unmeasurable wailing and howling, and could speak unto thee, without all doubt he himself would rebuke it, and say:

97

"Why will you vex your age with unprofitable, yea, with unreasonable mourning? Wherefore will you blame God, his ordinance, and providence? Will ye envy me the great honour and joy that I am promoted unto? Think ye it is a thing to be bewailed and lamented, that I am brought out of danger into safeguard, out of misery into welfare, and out of the wicked world into the company of angels? I will go somewhat nearer unto you: I pray you, if it lay in your strength and power to send for me into the temporal life again, would ye call me down again into the misery of yours? With what great fault have I deserved such unfaithfulness at your hands? And if ye should not call me again, why mourn ye then so and lament?" Upon such words, we must needs be ashamed of our unmeasurable sorrow and heaviness. That we ought thus to judge of faithful christian men that are departed, we may learn by the words

John xi. of Christ, who testifieth unto Martha: "I am the resurrection and the life. He that believeth on me shall live, although he die; and he that liveth and believeth on me, shall never

Psal. cxvi. die." "How dear and precious in the sight of the Lord is the death of his saints!" Understand, that God doth faithfully take them into his protection, and hath respect unto their souls, to receive them into eternal life.

Now sayest thou: Alas! if I knew that my wife, child, or friend were saved, I could then better away with his death. As for a thief, he need not to be glad, when he is carried from prison to the gallows. This man hath been all his life a child of the world; he never feared God, but died in sin, haply without repentance, and peradventure from the cart of this misery he is yoked in the chariot of eternal fire.

Answer: no man can tell, how he behaved himself at his last end: happily he repented, and is pardoned. We ought ever to hope the best, till we have sufficient evidences that the man is lost.

Secondly: though his damnation were open and manifest, yet ought a faithful man to rejoice in the righteousness of God. The ravens must have dog's garbage; partridges must be set upon the board before lords; a murderer must be laid upon a wheel. It is as meet for Judas to sit in hell, as for St Peter to be in heaven.

Thirdly, thou sayest: if he had lived longer, he would peradventure have amended. Whereupon take this answer: he might have happened as soon to be worse. A prudent man looketh for no better, but feareth the worse in this blasphemous world.

St John Chrysostom testifieth plainly, that "as soon as God taketh away a man through death, the same man from thenceforth should never have been better[1]."

Verily, God is to be praised and thanked, when he taketh away the ungodly. For the more a man heapeth up sin upon sin, the greater punishment must he suffer afterward, for God's righteous justice sake. The ungodly sinneth ever the longer, the more upon earth: but by death doth God pluck him down from his sinful life; though not spiritually and inwardly, yet with external members, the same must cease from sin. Therefore to such as are hard-hearted and disordered, there is nothing better than to die the sooner.

CHAPTER III.

WHAT PROFIT THE DEATH OF FRIENDS BRINGETH TO SUCH AS ARE LEFT BEHIND ALIVE.

THAT the death of the ungodly doth profit other men, it is easy to perceive; for thereby are the wicked upon earth somewhat diminished and swept out, and other poor wretches fare the better.

But that the death of the righteous should bring any commodity to such as remain alive, it soundeth strange in our ears: therefore shall it be declared.

When a man endowed with excellent gifts is made an idol, Almighty God cannot suffer it. For God himself will be he, of whom all good things undoubtedly must be hoped and looked for; and unto his dishonour it serveth, if the heart cleave not only unto him. And blessed is the man, that setteth his love, comfort, and hope upon the Lord. Again, "Cursed be the man," as the prophet saith, "that [Jer. xvii.] upon man doth put his trust." Now cometh it lightly to

[1 The sentiment is found in Chrysostom, Homil. ad Matthæum xxxi. in fine. Opera, Tom. vii. p. 364. B. Ed. Paris. 1727.]

pass, that we set too much by rich parents, by fair children, honourable friends, and men of good properties. Therefore God plucketh them away from us, to draw us away from creatures, and that we might perceive his fervent love towards us, in that he is jealous over us, that he taketh out of our sight whatsoever we gape upon besides himself; and also to the intent that we might perceive, that whatsoever is in the world, it is but temporal, and lasteth but the twinkling of an eye; and that only the Father of heaven will, can, and may help in all troubles.

Moreover, what a number is there of them, that of an inordinate love toward their children, parents, and friends, to make provision for them, and to bring them aloft, jeopard their souls for them, fall into great unquietness, being unmerciful, covetous, bribers, usurers, liars, deceivers! Franciscus Petrarcha writeth: "Thou hast lost thy son; yea, but thou hast lost with him also much fear, and an infinite matter of careful sorrows: by reason of the which cares, that thou mightest be delivered from them, it behoved either thee or thy son to die."

Therefore give God thanks for his grace, when he dischargeth thee of those things that hinder thee in his free service; and when he taketh from thee thy wife, child, friend, or others upon whom thou hast hanged too much, and for whose sakes thou hast done wrong many a time.

That thou mayest understand this thing the better, take for example mercy towards the poor. We see that they whose children and friends are departed give alms richly, which while their wives, children, and friends were alive, would not have given one penny, for fear that their friends after their death should have had need, and been destitute of money themselves. Yea, rich folks, which, as God sometime appointeth, have no children, nor heirs of their own bodies, become fathers and upholders of many poor men. Which thing unto them and unto all Christendom is more profitable and more worthy of commendation, than ten sons of a naughty life, such as commonly there be many: among whom scarce one of ten speedeth well, I mean of those that inherit their father's riches and goods; for shamefully they waste and consume them, to the hurt of themselves and of others.

Item, though one know that he ought to love no man in such sort, as to displease God for his sake; yet many a time is one moved through his friends to do against his own conscience, if he will not displease them. Therefore graciously doth God pluck away those friends, whose presence serveth unto thy destruction.

Moreover thou sayest: How should not I mourn, seeing I am now robbed of such help and succour, as I should still have, if he were yet alive? Answer: such complaining cometh not of a free love towards the dead, but of a servile and bond stomach, that looketh and hath respect to itself, and desireth to work his own profit with another man's hurt. Now if thy son or friend, that might have been thy comfort in thine age, be departed, God may send thee others in their place; yea, there be some at hand already, that offer their help and counsel to thee and thine, and will not fail thee at thy need. And though it were so, that thou hadst none other child nor friend in their stead, but were destitute of all bodily help; yet hast thou a gracious God through Jesus Christ, with the spiritual gifts which shall continue with thee for ever.

But some say, and especially great youngsters, My mourning and sorrow is because my kindred, name, and stock, mine arms and badge perisheth, now that I leave no heirs of my body behind me. O thou great idiot! thou lamentest that thy name and honour perisheth in this transitory world, and forcest little, how thy name and honour may continue for evermore in the kingdom of heaven.

What is become of the mighty kings and emperors, which fought for the greatest honour and magnificence, that they might never be forgotten upon earth? The memorial of them is past long ago; they have their reward already, as our Lord sayeth. Contrariwise, the dear worthy saints, which despised all glory of this mortal life, have at this day greater honour, praise, and commendation, than they that travailed to obtain the glory of this world. Now therefore will God help thee, not to pass upon temporal honour and pomp; but most of all to care, how thy name may remain in remembrance before God, with those that unto him have done faithful service.

CHAPTER IV.

COMPANIONS THAT SUFFER LIKE HEAVINESS OF HEART.

IF any thing were practised against thy child or friend, that necessarily must not come to pass, so that he might well have escaped it, then hadst thou just cause to howl and lament. But now behoved it him, as a mortal man, to end this life even according to the first ordinance of God. Thou hast thousands and thousands of companions, whose dear friends departed hence by death : why wilt thou then disquiet thyself? What time as Abraham was commanded of God to sacrifice his own only beloved son, what mind had he, thinkest thou, when he now drew the sword, and thought to slay his son? Greater sorrow had he for his son that yet was alive, than thou for thy son that is dead. In what case was the holy patriarch Jacob's heart, when tidings came to him, that his dear son Joseph was torn of wild beasts? Where was there ever father in greater heaviness than even David, when by his own son Absalom, whom he yet exceedingly loved, he was expelled from his kingdom? Doubtless he was in none other case, than as though the heart in his body shrunk and melted like wax. These and such like examples oughtest thou to set before thine eyes ; whereby thou shalt perceive, that thy sorrow is to be esteemed but small towards these ; and therefore through the contemplation thereof undoubtedly it shall be assuaged.

CHAPTER V.

THROUGH GOD'S HELP ALL HEART-SORROW IS EASED.

UNHANDSOME physicians are they, that well can see the greatness of the sickness, and brawl with the patient for his excess, but cannot shew a remedy whereby the blemish may be healed. Therefore now that I have hitherto reproved unmeasurable sorrow and heaviness, I will not leave the matter so bare ; but declare now also a medicine, whereby unreasonable mourning, if it be not clean taken away, may yet be eased and diminished.

The time of itself maketh all cumbrance lighter. For there be many men and women which in times past have set finger in the eye, knocked upon their breasts, pulled the hair out of their own heads, run against the wall, disfigured their whole bodies, and horribly howled for the dead. But now they have their pastime in all kinds of minstrelsy, as though they never had ailed anything. Notwithstanding to wait still till heaviness forget itself, is a womanish thing : and again, to bridle it betimes, beseemeth the natural reason and soberness of a man. What is then to be done ? It lieth not in thy power, without the special help of God, to expel sorrowful mourning. First and principally, ponder thou the power and grace of God : the power, in that the Almighty is able many hundred ways faithfully to ease thee of thy sorrow ; the grace, in that he is willing and ready, for the worthiness of his Son, to make thee joyful again here and in the world to come, so as is most for thy profit and wealth. Adam and Eve had unspeakable sorrow, when their obedient and righteous son Abel was murdered : God then did well put them in remembrance of their sin. But they being also mindful of the promise of the blessed Seed, were thereby erected and comforted again : howbeit in such an exceeding heaviness it was very hard to withstand desperation, and to overcome all mischance. Therefore let us consider, that though we Christians be not altogether called to the pleasures of this time, but stoutly to strive and valiantly to fight against them ; yet shall not Christ leave us comfortless, but, according to his promise, he shall faithfully be with us unto the end of the world.

CHAPTER VI.

WE MUST FURNISH OURSELVES WITH PRAYER AND PATIENCE.

To the intent that God may assist us with his might and grace, we must earnestly pray unto him, that with his holy Spirit through his godly word he will comfort us, that we may render thanks unto him when he hath delivered our friends from the daily battle of the soul against the flesh, the devil, and the world, and from all discommodities of this vale of misery.

For like as one that hath fared well at a dinner, doth thank his host, though the host let him depart again, yea, the guest rejoiceth afterwards to remember it; even so, forasmuch as God for a season hath lent us wife, child, and friends (which is more than he owed us), though he suffer them to depart, we ought nevertheless to give him most high thanks.

Especially there is required a willing and stout mind: whereof holy St Paul hath written this very comfortably: 1 Thess. iv. " I would not, brethren, that ye should be ignorant concerning them which are fallen asleep, that ye sorrow not as other do which have no hope. For if we believe that Jesus died and rose again, even so them also which sleep by Jesus will God bring again with him."

By these words may we perceive, that there be two manner of mourners for the dead. The heathen and unbelievers mourn without hope of the resurrection: their opinion is, that seeing their near friends are dead, there is no more of them, but that they have utterly lost them for ever. This heathenish sorrow will not St Paul have of Christians.

The Christians mourn also, but with a living hope of the joyful resurrection. For like as God the Father left not Christ the Lord in death, but raised him up again, and placed him in eternal life; even so us that believe shall not he leave in death, but bring us out into everlasting life. For this cause doth the Apostle speak of the dead, as of those that sleep, which rest from all travail and labour, that they may rise again in better case.

Like as the flowers with all their virtue, smell, and beauty, lieth all the winter in the root, sleeping and resting till they be awaked with the pleasant time of May, when they come forth with all their beauty, smell, and virtue; even so ought not we to think that our friends which be departed are in any cumbrance or sorrow, but their strength and virtue being drawn in, liveth in God and with God. They lie and rest till the last day, when they shall awake again, fair, beautiful, and glorious, in soul and body. Who will not now rejoice at this comfort of Paul, and set aside all unprofitable sorrow, for this exceeding joy's sake?

Faith that is confessed with the mouth, must not be destroyed with a contrary deed. Now is our belief set thus: " I believe forgiveness of sins, the resurrection of the body, and the life everlasting." Therefore remaineth there nothing behind, for the which the soul of the faithful should be tormented in the world to come, or shut out from everlasting joy. In the law xiii. 9, 2, *Ubicunque*, it is noted: " Unseemly heaviness for the dead springeth out of despair of the resurrection for to come; and rather of faintness of mind, than of mercy or godliness[1]."

CHAPTER VII.

ENSAMPLES OF PATIENCE IN LIKE CASE.

If the wise famous heathen could be numbered, which took the death of their friends and children in good part and with a stout stomach, should it not be counted a shame unto us christian men, that declare less constancy in that behalf?

Pericles, the captain of the Athenians (who for his wisdom and virtue was called Olympius, one of heaven), when he had lost his two sons, Paralius and Zantippus, within the space of four days, was no more sorry nor unquieted in the same sudden chance, but that on the day following he came clothed in white before the whole multitude, and consulted of the present wars so discreetly and manfully, that every man wondered at him and honoured him[2].

Xenophon, a disciple of Socrates, when he understood that his only son Gryllus had fought valiantly, and upon the same was slain of the enemies, he said unto those that brought him the message: " I made my prayer unto the gods, not that they should give me an immortal son, or that he might be a long liver, (for I knew not whether that were profitable for him,) but that of my son they would make a good man, and a lover of his own native country; which

[1 Lugere autem et deplorare et lamentari eos, qui de hac vita decedunt, ex pusillanimitate contingit. Hoc autem ex desperatione futuræ resurrectionis intelligitur. Corpus Juris Canon. Tom. I. p. 1042. Ed. Lugd. 1661.]
[2 Valerius Maximus, Lib. v. cap. 10.]

prayer, as I perceive, they have granted; and therefore I thank them[1]."

If thou hadst rather hear examples of the Romans, then consider Paulus Emilius, who overcame the Macedonians, and triumphed gloriously over them. When he within seven days had lost both his sons, he was not therefore broken-minded; but as he went forth to the multitude without both his sons, (which beforetime always led him and stayed him, the one on the right hand, the other on the left,) the people of Rome, having pity on the old honourable man, began to lament and weep. But he, being nothing moved, stood there and said: " I besought the gods, if our commonwealth, for the great prosperity thereof, have any evil will among those which be in heaven, that I myself, and not the whole multitude, might recompense and bear it: and seeing it is so, I give God great thanks[2]." M. Fabius Maximus also, not without just cause, belongeth unto the number of dear worthy men. When he upon a time had to do with the office of the master of works, there came unto him a message, first, that his house was fallen down, and had also bruised his wife, a virtuous honourable woman; secondly, slain his mother, who in weighty affairs had oft given him good counsel, which he followed to the great commodity of the commonwealth: thirdly, it was told him the same day, that his young son, of whom he had an expectation and hope of all goodness, was dead in Umbria. The friends and lovers of this Fabius, that stood about him, when they heard this, wept very sore: but he alone being unmoved, went forward stoutly in the business that concerned the commonwealth[3].

[1 Valer. Max. Ibid.]

[2 The circumstances of this history are related by Livy, Lib. XLV. c. xl. xli. Postquam omnia secundo navium cursu in Italiam peryenerant, neque erat quod ultra precarer; illud optavi, ut quum ex summo retro volvi fortuna consuesset, mutationem ejus domus mea potius quam respublica sentiret. Itaque defunctam esse fortunam publicam mea tam insigni calamitate spero. Compare also Valer. Max. Lib. v. cap. 10.]

[3 It does not appear from what source the learned writer has borrowed this history. Plutarch, in his life of Fabius Maximus, (ed. Bryan. 1729. Vol. I. p. 407), relates the account of the fortitude of Fabius on the death of his son; but omits all mention of the other circumstances of the history.]

Here, because of shortness, I leave out a multitude of examples of sundry men, named Galli, Pisones, Scævolæ, Metelli, Scauri, Marcelli; whom in such points to follow, it is laudable and worthy of commendation.

I will yet shew one example, of the virtuous woman Cornelia, which was daughter unto Scipio Africanus. When she understood that her two sons, Tiberius Gracchus and C. Gracchus (who, being magistrates, had honourably and well behaved themselves), were slain, and she of her friends was called miserable, she said: "I will never think myself a miserable woman, forasmuch as I have brought forth such men[4]."

This woman now overcame her own natural feebleness and motherly heart: should not then a man (which word noteth the stronger kind and more valiant stomach) declare himself even as stout? That an heathenish unbelieving woman could despise, should that make a faithful christian man so utterly faint-hearted? That she willingly gave again unto nature, wilt not thou suffer God to have it, when he requireth it of thee? She took upon her, with an unbroken mind, the death of many children; and wilt not thou, that foregoest but one child, be comforted again? The heathenish woman knew none other, but that after death there remaineth nothing behind; yet made not she an unmeasurable howling. Thou knowest that after this time there remaineth an everlasting life: so much the worse then beseemeth it a christian man to unquiet himself with excess of heaviness.

CHAPTER VIII.

THE COMMODITY OF PATIENCE.

UNSEEMLY sorrow for their sakes that are dead is unprofitable and hurtful. Unprofitable: for as soon as the soul is once departed out of the body, it cometh either into heaven or into hell, and with no crying shall it be called back again, or altered. Neither canst thou serve the dead with any thing more, than that his remembrance be dear

[4 See Plutarch, Vit. C. Gracchi. Vol. IV. p. 400. ed. Bryan.]

and had in honour with thee. The heathenish poet Sophocles writeth : "If the dead might with tears be called again, then should weeping be counted more worthy than gold. But, O my good old man, it may not be, that he which once is buried should come again to the light. For if weeping might help, my father had been alive again[1]." Hurtful: hereof hath the heathenish poet Philemon written right wisely : "Many of them through their own fault increase misfortune to themselves, and make the same more grievous than it is of nature. Example : when one hath his mother, child, or friend dead, if he thought thus, He was a man, and therefore he died ; this adversity should be no greater, than nature bringeth with it. But if he cry, 'I am undone, I shall see him no more, he is gone and lost for ever;' such one heapeth up yet more sorrow to that he hath already. But whoso considereth everything with discretion, maketh the adversity to be less unto himself, and obtaineth the more quietness[2]."

It were a very scornful thing, if when a man hath hurt one foot, he would therefore mar the other also ; or if, when one part of his goods is stolen away, he would cast the rest

[1 This passage is found amongst the Fragments of Sophocles, and is taken from the lost play of the ΣΚΥΡΙΑΙ :

Ἀλλ' εἰ μὲν ἦν κλαίουσιν ἰᾶσθαι κακά,
καὶ τὸν θανόντα δακρύοις ἀνιστάναι,
ὁ χρυσὸς ἦσσον κτῆμα τοῦ κλαίειν ἂν ἦν.
νῦν δ', ὦ γεραιὲ, ταῦτ' ἀνηνύτως ἔχει,
τὸν μὲν τάφῳ κρυφθέντα πρὸς τὸ φῶς ἄγειν·
κἀμοὶ γὰρ ἂν πατήρ γε δακρύων χάριν
ἀνῆκτ' ἂν εἰς φῶς.

Sophocl. ed. Brunck. Vol. II. pp. 51, 52.]

[2 Μείζω τὰ κακὰ ποιοῦσι πολλοί, δέσποτα,
αὐτοὶ δι' αὑτοὺς, ἢ πέφυκε τῇ φύσει.
οἷον, τέθνηκεν υἱὸς ἢ μήτηρ τινὶ,
ἢ νὴ Δί' ἄλλων τῶν ἀναγκαίων γέ τις·
εἰ μὲν λάβῃ τοῦτ', Ἀπέθαν', ἄνθρωπος γὰρ ἦν,
τοσοῦτο γέγονε τὸ κακὸν, ἡλίκον περ ἦν.
ἐὰν δ', Ἀβίωτος ὁ βίος, οὐκ ἔτ' ὄψομαι,
ἀπόλωλ',—ἐν ἑαυτῷ τοῦτ' ἐὰν σκοπῇ, κακὰ
πρὸς τοῖς κακοῖσιν οὗτος ἕτερα συλλέγει.
ὁ δὲ τῷ λογισμῷ πάντα παρ' ἑαυτῷ σκοπῶν
τὸ κακὸν ἀφαιρεῖ, τἀγαθὸν δὲ λαμβάνει.

Philemon ap. Stobæi Florileg. Tom. III. p. 379, ed. Gaisford.]

into the sea, and say that he so bewaileth his adversity. No less foolishly do they, that enjoy not such goods as are present, and regard not their friends that be alive; but spoil and mar themselves, because their wives, children, or friends, be departed.

Though one of the husbandman's trees doth wither away, he heweth not down therefore all the other trees; but regardeth the other so much the more, that they may win the thing again, which the other lost. Even so learn thou in adversity, with such goods as are left thee to comfort and refresh thyself again.

CHAPTER IX.

WE OUGHT SO TO LOVE OUR CHILDREN AND FRIENDS, THAT WE MAY FORSAKE THEM.

ALL such things ought of us to be considered, taken in hand, and exercised, while our wives and friends are still alive. Namely, if thou have father or mother, husband or wife, child or friends, lay not thine heart, love, and affection too much upon them, how good, profitable, and honest soever they be; but remember alway that they are transitory things, which thou mayest lose and forego, when time requireth. Love him most of all, whom thou canst not lose, even thy Redeemer; who, to draw thee unto his love, and to deliver thee from the love of the world, stretched out his arms, and suffered the most vile death for thee upon the cross.

Love thy friends, because God hath commanded thee to love them, and not for affection to them, and then wilt thou be contented with God's good will and pleasure.

Seneca saith not unwisely: "I lend myself unto the things of the world, but I do not give myself to them." He saith moreover, that "nothing is possessed as it ought to be, except one be ready at all times to lose it."

Note the saying of an heathen man then greatly to our shame.

But if we fasten our hearts (so to say) upon our children and friends; that is, if we love them too much, and not God above all things; then hath our sorrow no measure as ought, as they are altered or taken away. Therefore if thou hast not prepared thyself to adversity by times, and art once overtaken with indiscreet heaviness, then let it be unto thee a warning from henceforth to keep thee from the greater love of transitory things, which hath brought thee into such heart-sorrow; to the intent that at other times thou mayest take the death of thy wife and children in good part, and with more constancy of mind.

CHAPTER X.

OF THE DEATH OF YOUNG PERSONS IN ESPECIAL.

AFTER the general instruction concerning death, must certain objections be answered that hitherto are not resolved. If a young man, or if a young daughter die, Lord, what a great mourning beginneth there to be! 'Alas! he is taken away in his young days before his time; he should first have been married, and had a good wife upon earth, and in his last age have died in peace and rest.' Hereof cometh it that we think the death of children to be unnatural, even as when the flame of fire through water is violently quenched. The death of the aged we think to be natural, as when the fire quencheth of itself, according to the saying of Cicero[1].

Item, the death of young persons is compared to unripe apples, that with violence are plucked off from the tree: the death of the aged is thought to be, as when ripe apples fall down of themselves.

Item, as it is hard to undo two boards newly glued together, but old joinings are lightly broken asunder; so we complain that young folks die with greater pain than the old: yea, it grieveth the father's and mother's heart, when, as they count it, that matter is turned upside down, that children depart out of this world before old folks. The answer is taken out of the before rehearsed ground. If God, who hath all in his own power, had promised every one a long life, then mightest thou complain at the shortening of the life of thyself or of thy friends against God's promise. Now hath God compared and clothed the soul with the body, that what day or what twinkling of an eye soever he commandeth it to depart, it keepeth the same time wherein one finisheth his course. Therefore hath no man cause to complain of an untimely death; but look, whatsoever one hath lived over and beside the first day of his birth, it is an increase.

The will of God.

The shortness of this time.

[1 De Senectute. c. 19.]

110

Moreover, God knoweth much better than thou and we all, when it is best for every one to die. And so faithful is he for the Lord Jesus Christ's sake, that he in no wise will be too hasty upon us.

Secondly, though we remain a long season in this fickle transitory life, yet is all our time but short, specially towards the endless eternity. Therefore it hath but a slender difference, to depart hence in youth, or in age.

Thirdly, through death is a young person withdrawn away from many troubles, which else were at his door. For commonly, the longer a man liveth, the more miserable is he.

Take examples out of old stories. If Themistocles, after the most glorious victory against Xerxes, when all the Greeks acknowledged and commended him for their redeemer and deliverer, had died, should it not have served him to a perpetual praise and honour? Then should not he afterward have been rated as a betrayer of Greece; then needed not he to have been in bondage, nor to have fallen down at the foot of the king of Barbary, as before a God, whom he before had driven out of Greece. How thrall and vile a thing was it to be esteemed before the world, that Themistocles must needs come before king Xerxes!

What is to be said of Marcus Cicero, who confesseth himself, that if he had died sooner, he had escaped exceeding great troubles? And forasmuch as he so said, while the matter was yet tolerable; how would he first have thought and lamented in his age, to see with his eyes the drawn swords over the senators' and citizens' heads, and when the most principal men's goods were parted among murderers; yea, when, whereas beforetime there was one Catiline, the city was now become full of such seditious persons! *Catiline was a seditious man.*

The examples of daily experience declare sufficiently before our eyes, whereby we may evidently perceive, that death, though they call it untimely, delivereth yet from great misfortune and adversity.

Fourthly, the innocency and cleanness of youth is of their own nature, and through evil example, defiled and stained with the life and conversation that followeth after. Augustine saith, "The older the worse[2]."

[2 The following passage appears to contain the sentiment of Augustine, which is here referred to: Quisquis igitur es amator vitæ

111

Therefore when a young man falleth on sleep, know thou that God sheweth great grace unto him, in that he suffereth him not, as many other, to remain long in this blasphemous world, to the intent he should no more be hindered and defiled with it; but hath called him from hence to a right good state, that with himself and all the elect he might possess the kingdom of heaven. Witness of the scripture: " Suddenly was he taken away, to the intent that wickedness should not alter his understanding. His soul pleased God, therefore hasted he to take him away from among the wicked."

He speaketh of Henoch. Wisd. iv.

Similitudes. He that is upon the sea, and with a good strong wind is carried soon to the haven or land where he would be, is happier than he, that for lack of wind is fain to sail still many years and days upon the sea with much trouble and weariness. Even so the more happy is he, whom death taketh away from the stormy and raging sea of this world. Seeing there is set before us an universal native country, and he that is long in going thither, obtaineth no more than he that is speedily gone thither before-hand; should not one wish, that he had soon overcome the foul dangerous way that leadeth to the heavenly harbour?

The sooner one payeth his debt, the better it is. If there were none other remedy, but that with an hundred more thou must needs be beheaded, and thou art the first that is put to execution, art thou not then the first that is despatched of the pain?

Finally, if thou consider the mischances of other folks, thou hast the less cause to complain. One dieth in the mother's womb, before he be born. Another dieth in the very birth. The third in his flourishing youth, when he first delighteth to live, falleth away as a beautiful rose. Among a thousand is there not one that cometh to the perfect age.

longæ, esto potius bonæ vitæ. Nam si male vivere volueris, longa vita non erit verum bonum, sed erit longum malum. August. de Verbis Apostol. Homil. I. Opera, Vol. x. p. 90. G. Ed. 1541.]

CHAPTER XI.

OF THE DEATH OF THE AGED.

WHEN old aged folks are greedy of this wretched life, they do even as those that, when the wine is all spent, will needs drink out the wine-lees also. Whoso dwelleth in an old rotten house that sinketh down, needeth not long to seek props to underset it, but should rather be glad to get him out of it: even so old aged folks, by reason of their decayed body, should rather be content to depart from it. And this advantage they have, that their death is not so fierce and painful as the death of young folks.

This is chiefly to be considered, that the Lord our God will not have us careful, (which thing belongeth unto him alone,) but to be faithful and true, and diligently to labour. Old fathers and mothers are not able to travail any more; and yet with earnest carefulness they think to bring all things to pass. This special fault they have, that they think they shall ever lack. Therefore unto them verily it is best, that God take them away from all care, sorrow, and trouble, and place them in quiet rest with other faithful christian folks.

CHAPTER XII.

OF STRANGE DEATH.

WHOSO is taken with the pestilence, or dieth else of sickness in his bed, ought gladly to suffer the hand of God; for everybody hath deserved a far worse death. And a very small rod is this towards it that God sendeth over the ungodly, yea, ofttimes over his own dear children, when one is beheaded, another burned, the third drowned, &c.; where they altogether may sing with David: "For thy sake are we killed every day, and counted as sheep appointed to be slain." But if one die an unwonted death, (as one is destroyed by the hangman, another dieth a sudden death, the third, as happily a man's child falleth down dead from an

Ps. xliv.
Rom. viii.
2 Cor. iv.

high place,) this take we for a terrible death, and cannot tell else what to say of it; as though every kind of death in itself were not terrible unto the nature of man. Though one dieth upon the wheel for murder, there is sometime more hope of him, that he hath found grace at God's hand, than of many one that dieth at home in his bed. Examples also are to be considered: for a great sort of God's elect died not a right death, as we use to term it. Abel was murdered of his own natural brother. The prophet, being sent to Jeroboam, was destroyed of a lion. Isaiah was sawn asunder through the middle. Jeremiah, like as Steven also, was stoned to death. James, being thrown down from the pulpit, was slain of a fuller[1]. Peter at Rome was fastened to a cross. Upon Paul was execution done with the sword[2]. Such like examples hast thou.

Heb. xi.

Item, the most excellent heathen men came miserably out of this world. The good Socrates was poisoned; Euripides was all-to torn of dogs; Sophocles was choked with a little stone of a grape berry; very sorrowful cumbrance did fret out the heart of Homer. Innumerable examples declare, that there happeneth no new thing unto us, what death soever we or our friends die.

Especially let us observe this rule: death is terrible to them that have no God; but of us that are God's children ought not the horrible image of death to be feared, but to be welcome unto us. For God himself comforteth us with these words following: "I live, and ye also shall live." Of this are we assured in Christ Jesu, who upon the cross died the most horrible death for our sakes: to whom with the Father, and the Holy Ghost, be all honour and glory for ever and ever. Amen.

John xiv.

Only unto God give the praise.

[1 Euseb. Hist. Eccles. Lib. II. c. 23. p. 30. ed. Reading, 1720; and Hegesippi Fragmenta apud Routh. Rel. Sacr. Vol. I. p. 195.]
[2 With respect to the martyrdom of St Peter and St Paul, compare Euseb. Hist. Eccles. Lib. II. c. 25. p. 83. S. Petri Alexandrini Fragmenta apud Routh. Rel. Sacr. Vol. III. p. 332; and Pearson. Annales Paulini ad annum Christi 68, Neronis 14.]

AN EXHORTATION WRITTEN BY THE LADY JANE,
THE NIGHT BEFORE SHE SUFFERED, IN THE
END OF THE NEW TESTAMENT IN
GREEK, WHICH SHE SENT TO
HER SISTER, LADY
KATHARINE.

I HAVE here sent you, good sister Katherine, a book; which although it be not outwardly trimmed with gold, yet inwardly it is more worth than precious stones. It is the book, dear sister, of the law of the Lord; it is his testament and last will, which he bequeathed to us wretches, which shall lead you to the path of eternal joy. And if you with a good mind read it, and with an earnest desire follow it, it shall bring you to an immortal and everlasting life. It will teach you to live, and learn you to die; it shall win you more than you should have gained by the possessions of your woeful father's lands. For as, if God had prospered him, you should have inherited his lands; so if you apply diligently this book, seeking to direct your life after it, you shall be an inheritor of such riches, as neither the covetous shall withdraw from you, neither the thief shall steal, neither yet the moths corrupt.

Desire with David, good sister, to understand the law of the Lord your God. Live still to die; that you by death may purchase eternal life, or after your death enjoy the life purchased you by Christ's death. And trust not, that the tenderness of your age shall lengthen your life: for as soon, if God call, goeth the young as the old. And labour alway to learn to die, deny the world, defy the devil, and despise the flesh, and delight yourself only in the Lord. Be penitent for your sins, and yet despair not. Be strong in faith, and yet presume not. And desire with St Paul to be dissolved and to be with Christ, with whom even in death there is life. Be like the good servant, and even at midnight be waking; lest when death cometh and stealeth upon you, like a thief in the night, you be with the evil servant found sleeping; and lest for lack of oil ye be found like the five foolish women, and like him that had not on the wedding-garment; and then be cast out from the marriage. Rejoice in Christ, as I trust ye do. And seeing ye have the name of a Christian, as near as ye can, follow the steps of your master Christ, and take up your cross, lay your sins on his back, and always embrace him. And as touching my death, rejoice as I do, good sister, that I shall be delivered of this corruption, and put on incorruption. For I am assured that I shall, for losing of a mortal life, win an immortal life. The which I pray God grant you; send you of his grace to live in his fear, and to die in the true christian faith: from the which, in God's name, I exhort you that you neither swerve, neither for hope of life, nor fear of death. For if ye will deny his truth to lengthen your life, God will deny you, and yet shorten your days. And if ye will cleave to him, he will prolong your days to your comfort and his glory. To the which glory God bring me now, and you hereafter, when it shall please God to call you! Farewell, good sister, and put your only trust in God, who only must help you.

Your loving sister,
JANE DUDLEY.

Glossary

This glossary gives words and phrases that are likely to cause difficulty to modern readers. Within the book, the Parker Society editor also added footnotes defining expressions that were obsolete in the 19th century.

again	in return (i.e., back again).
approved of God	proven, shown, or attested by God.
away with(al)	put up with or get along with.
battery	Apparent meaning: besiegement.
bewray, verb	to divulge secrets; to discredit a person by exposing his secrets or sins; more generally, to reveal, make known, show.
brawl (with), verb	contend (with), scold.
burghership	citizenship.
captain	leader.
cast, verb	ponder, deliberate.
certify (someone)	make (a person) certain or sure (*of* a matter); to assure, inform certainly.
comfort, verb	The old meaning included strengthening a person's spirit or resolve and/or strengthening physically, as well as providing solace.
comfortable	able to give comfort, comforting.
commodity	benefit, convenience, advantage, or interest.

conceit	according to the context: notion, opinion, sometimes frame of mind or disposition.
conditions	characteristics.
convenient	befitting, proper.
conversation	life, manner of life, way of living.
crack, verb	brag, sometimes with sense of scorn toward others. Past form 'crake.'
dainty	particular about comfort and luxury.
despise, verb	hate, scorn, or hold in contempt; more weakly, neglect or ignore.
despite	contemptuous and injurious attitude or action.
dispatch, verb	perform, get through.
doctrine	in some contexts, a lesson or piece of instruction.
dote, verb	become mentally weak or impaired.
effectuous	effectual.
fain	in "would fain": would gladly, would like to.
finger's end	In "to have (something) on his finger's end" = to have at his fingertips.
fly, verb	flee, escape away.
force (little), verb	care (little).
forsake, verb	let go, without any sense of abandonment.
froward	habitually contrary, rebellious. More generally, evilly inclined.
furnish, verb	supply, provide, prepare; sometimes, adorn.
ghostly	spiritual.
glass	hourglass.

godly	divine, as in "godly power" or "godly wisdom."
hale, verb	pull, drag.
happen of course	happen as a matter of course.
harness	defensive armour or equipment, military accoutrement. See also 'ordnance' and 'gear.'
health	salvation.
keep, verb	guard, protect, watch over.
knowledge, verb	acknowledge.
linger, verb	delay, put off.
lovers	loving friends.
lust, noun or verb	wish or desire.
lusty, lustily	according to the context: willing, strong, valiant, vigorous, desirous. Also pleasing (as in "lusty to the eyes"). Whence *lustily*: willingly, valiantly, etc.
meaning	understanding, opinion, belief.
meat	food, sustenance.
meddle (with), verb	to concern or occupy oneself with or in a matter. The sense of undue interference was not usually present in older use.
naughty	according to the context: worthless, morally bad, or blameworthy.
noise, verb	tell widely as a report or rumour.
noisome	harmful, noxious; more weakly, annoying.
notify (to), verb	tell, inform.
nurture	upbringing or education.

only	single or one and only. Now often expressed by 'alone' placed after the phrase modified.
open, verb	according to the context: declare, reveal, disclose, or show.
ordnance	armour, weapons, and military supplies. See also 'harness' and 'gear.'
original	origin, fount, or source.
parcel	component part or member.
pass upon, verb	regard.
prevent, verb	go before.
prince	high ruler.
publish, verb	declare widely, make known abroad.
reasonable	reasoning; capable of reasoning.
save, verb	in some contexts, safeguard or preserve.
scholars	students.
science	knowledge; also a field of study.
sentence	judgement or meaning.
stomach	used like 'heart' or 'breast' to indicate the inward seat of emotion, feelings, or secret thoughts.
stretch-leg	death.
target	a shield or buckler to ward off blows.
tell, verb	count (past form 'told' = counted).
temptation(s)	in some contexts, trial(s).
token	sign.

trow, verb	trust, believe. In "I trow (you)" = I trust, suppose, think, believe.
trusty	depending on the context, either trustworthy or trusting.
tutor	guardian, protector.
unhandsome	ill-suited.
unspeakable, unoutspeakable	indescribable, inexpressible. The present pejorative sense (indescribably bad or objectionable) did not develop until the 19th century.
utter, verb	reveal by deed or declare by word.
Vale	Farewell.
wealth	well-being, welfare.
were	In "it were" = "it would be."
which	= "who" in many contexts.
withal	with it all (in context here).
witty	wise or prudent; also skilful, intelligent.
wot, verb	know.
wroth	deep anger or resentment.

SCHEDULE B

The Apostles' Creed, which sets forth the foundational tenets of the Christian faith

Article 1: I believe in God the Father Almighty, Creator of heaven and earth,

Article 2: and in Jesus Christ his only Son, our Lord,

Article 3: who was conceived by the Holy Spirit and born of the virgin Mary.

Article 4: He suffered under Pontius Pilate, was crucified, dead, and buried.

Article 5: He descended into hell. The third day he arose again from the dead.

Article 6: He ascended into heaven and is seated at the right hand of God the Father Almighty.

Article 7: From thence he will come again to judge the living and the dead.

Article 8: I believe in the Holy Spirit,

Article 9: the holy catholic church, the communion of saints,

Article 10: the forgiveness of sins,

Article 11: the resurrection of the body,

Article 12: and the life everlasting.

Amen.

Lightning Source UK Ltd.
Milton Keynes UK
UKHW011956160921
390713UK00001B/25

9 781777 198770